Sorry Hillary!

GOD WANTS TRUMP!

In my humble opinion

NANCY MCLASKEY

Cataloging-in-Publication data on file with the Library of Congress

ISBN - 13: 978-1537072234

ISBN – 10: 1537072234

Ordering Information:

Quantity sales. Special discounts are available on quantity purchases by corporations, associations, or others. For details, contact the publisher at the email address listed above.

Printed in the United States of America

First Edition

CONTENTS

Introduction

How this book came to be. It all started during a primary Republican debate when Marco Rubio stated, "God willing, I will be the next President of the United States." Out of my mouth came the words, "Sorry Rubio, but God wants Trump." Whoa, wait one minute, where did that come from? I was a Democrat. I wasn't even registered to vote for a Republican. I have been a Democrat my entire life. I wasn't even a Trump fan. I was only watching the debate to see what all the hullabaloo was about. However, from that moment forward, as I went about my life, I couldn't shake the thought. And believe me, I tried. I'd push it aside. I'd tell myself no, I'm mistaken, and so on. Nevertheless, the thought lingered, so finally I said, "Ok, God if you want Donald Trump, then please help me to understand why, what do you see in this man that I don't? I promise, I will try my best to listen." The outcome of that is this book. It is as much about my faith-walk, and being faithful to the callings of God, as it is about the 2016 elections.

I am sure that because of this book, I will be attacked. I can already hear the snide comments.

"Well, God told me to vote for Hillary, so *who* do you think you are?"

"Really, God talks to you? Well, what should I have for lunch?"

> "Well, I'm a Never Trump supporter, and we prayed and know that God wants Evan McMullin, so you're flat-out wrong!"

And I'm sure the attacks will become even nastier and more threatening than this. I know that Trump supporters have posted pictures and online reports of being viscously attacked, as they walked to their cars, after attending a rally. And no they didn't start it. It's very sad that in a country, where we place such a high value on free speech, that such speech is only allowed to go one way. In fact, while promoting a movie in Dubai, Will Smith said that he was glad that Trump supporters spoke up because now, "We get to know who people are, and now we get to cleanse it out of our country." Does Will Smith realize that in the Muslim world to "cleanse it out" means to genocide an entire group of people? So, Will Smith wants me dead?

I know that Hillary Clinton is a devout Methodist. I was raised a Methodist. My grandparents were strong supporters of the Methodist movement, and founding members of a Methodist church in their home town. They also were the primary builders, donating both their time and money, to build a mountain retreat for their church's members and youth. My mother was a lay minister for the Methodist church. She was one of the early supporters, encouraging the Methodist church, to accept and support the LGBT community, because we have family members that belong to the LGBT community. I'm not questioning Hillary Clinton's faith. I'm sure Hillary Clinton prayed about this also. I'm not telling anyone whom to vote for. I'm just telling people who want to listen, my story, my faith-walk, that drew me to the conclusion of why, I believe, God wants Donald Trump as the next President of the United States of America.

One of the most important things, the next President of the United States will do, is nominate and appoint Supreme Court Justices. There is currently an opening for Scalia position, who was a conservative. Within the next four years, there could be up to three more openings. There could be one more conservative justice opening, if Kennedy, who is 80, retires. Along with two more liberal justices' openings, if Ginsburg who is 83 and battling cancer, and Breyer, who is 78, each retires. As we all know, each justice, does not interpret the Constitution the same. It is a "living document," and each case is subject to interpretation. One of the speakers at the DNC Convention, stated during his speech, that Hillary Clinton as President will be able to change the gun-control laws, by changing the face of the Supreme Court. As this statement, made at the DNC Convention, clearly shows, more than anything else, this election is about the ability of the 45th President to determine the type of justices appointed to the Supreme Court. The cases they hear and the decisions they make, will determine the America we live in for the next 30+ years.

Before this election, I knew very little about Donald Trump, I had only watched the Apprentice for part of one season. I got my news from ABC News, CNN, and sometimes the Internet. I knew even less about Bernie Sanders. However, as I started to evaluate Donald Trump, and as I listened to both Trump and Sanders, I began to realize that a lot of what they were saying was very similar. They both complained about money in politics, and the rigged system that results from it. They both talked about the country being run by the ultra-wealthy and the political elite/establishment. They both believed, that the Clintons have used our political system to line their own pockets and become very wealthy. They both complained about the need for new ways of approaching our problems. They both needed to fund their campaigns outside the traditional methods. And as we now know, they both were not supported by the mainstream, establishment, political parties. They both complained about NAFTA and the Trans-Pacific Partnership free trade agreements. They both want to handle illegal immigration and stop **illegal** immigrants from entering the United States. They both talked about how illegal immigrants keep wages low, and effects working-class Americans. Both Sanders and Trump, like the single-payer system of health care. Both were against the Iraq war, and both questioned the role of the U.S. as the policemen of the world. Both agreed that our infrastructure needs rebuilding and repairing. Both want fundamental change in this country. BUT, as we all know, their solutions are entirely different. Bernie Sanders wants Socialism and large giveaway programs. Donald Trump wants, among other things, the use of tariffs, along with income tax reform aimed at giving incentives to businesses and corporations to invest in America and create jobs in America.

The longer I prayed about it, investigated and researched the issues, the more I became convinced that we needed an outsider to shake up Washington and give America back to the people. I do not want our country to become a socialistic nation. The nations, usually cited and used by Bernie Sanders, in the past, to extoll the virtues of socialism, are Finland, Sweden, Norway, and Denmark. Of these four, Sweden, is the only one left that has a government headed by a socialist democracy. The other three countries have moved away from it. Venezuela is also a socialist democracy. On 7/2/16, Chuck Holtin of CBN News wrote an article called 'Real Hunger Games: This Country is Sliding into a Socialist Black Hole." In the article, he discussed all the problems they were having due to low oil prices and rampant corruption. The capital of Venezuela is considered the most violent city in the world. As a nation, why do we want to model ourselves off of something that sounds like a wonderful utopia, and yet, has failed country after country? Why do some people think it will work successfully for us, if it hasn't worked for the countries that have been trying it for a number of years?

I hope that you will read this book with an open mind and heart. You don't have to agree or even think as I do, but at least listen to the reasons, and develop your own opinion on them, as you decide who to vote for in the 2016

elections. Good luck to you all, and may God continue to
bless the United States of America.

How can a Democrat Really Be for Trump?

I am a college educated, retired women.

I have a Master's in Education.

I ~~am~~ was a Democrat.

I have been a voter for over 45 years.

I have voted in every Presidential

race since I became eligible to vote.

I should be voting for Hillary Clinton.

At least, per the political analysts, my demographics, and my own prior beliefs.

BUT this time

I AM VOTING FOR DONALD TRUMP.

It amazes even me!

As I have prayed about, researched, listened, watched, and thought, about this election, more than any other election in my life, I have come to believe with a strong conviction, that God wants Donald Trump to be the 45th President of the United States. I believe he created him with a special set of skills and experiences that is needed for this specific time in history. I know a lot of people will disagree with me. Even so, I also believe that a lot of other Americans are feeling the same discord and dissatisfaction with government, that I am. I believe our country needs certain changes right now, that only an outsider can bring about.

Up until this election cycle, I was a Democrat, and I was happy to be a Democrat. I really didn't pay a whole lot of attention to politics. I was busy living my life. But then, as stated in the introduction, my whole life changed, when I felt God telling me that he wanted Donald Trump for President, and he wanted me to write about it. Why does this matter? I have never done anything like this before. I do go through my day praying frequently about things, both big and small. I daily pray for guidance. I try to implement God's teaching into my life. I am a born-again Christian. I was baptized. I know that Christ lived and died on the cross for me. I know that God has a purpose for my life. Many times in the past, he has put me in the place where I needed to be, at the time I needed to be there. I try to use my God-given gifts to honor him. However, I have never before felt that I was being directed by God to do something political, and specific, like this in response to a political election.

In the beginning, I was scared. I delayed on the project and dragged my feet. Finally, when I couldn't ignore God's voice anymore, I began. I wrote a book, called A*rise America! It's Time for a Trumpertantrum.* I mailed out copies of the book, to certain people and media outlets. When I wrote the book, I used a pseudonym. I was afraid to use my real name. I was scared that people would harass my family. I was uncertain about the way that Trump tweeted and re-tweeted some offense tweets. I asked myself, "Were these the acts of a Godly man?" I was fearful that I was wrong, and that this wasn't what God wanted me to do. I was afraid to be faithful to God. I kept asking myself, why was I chosen? Why couldn't God find someone else to do this project? Why can't I just forget about this whole thing, and go on with my life?

I contacted the trumpertantrumclub.com website. I wrote several articles for it and tried to stay up to date on what was happening with the election. However, after my book had been for sale on Amazon for a week, we discovered typo errors in it. I was so afraid to tell anyone that I was doing a book, that I did all the editing myself. I missed things. So, I handed out copies of the book, gave it to people to edit and started mentioning to family members that I had written it. The response I got was happiness and excitement that I had written a book. And a lot of questionings, when I said it was about Donald Trump. Due to the typos and editing errors, I pulled the book. I was fully planning to correct the typos and put it back out there. But, then the nudging started again. I needed to do more than just correct the mistakes. I needed to add my story. I needed to add my faith-walk, and I NEEDED to put my real name on it. YIKES! REALLY GOD? REALLY? Oh boy.... Sometimes being faithful is hard. I kept asking myself, what about my family, what about my friends? What about my Hispanic friends? What about my Muslim friends? What about my liberal friends? What about my black friends? What about my female friends? What about my LGBT family members? After all, isn't everyone saying that Trump is against women, Hispanics, Muslims?

My husband and I strongly believe in diversity. When we had a choice of high schools to send our children to, we picked the school with the most diversity. We knew that it was essential for them to meet and interact and develop friendships with people from all ethnic backgrounds. This is the power and the blessing of America.

I didn't think I could do it. I didn't think I could be faithful to what I thought God wanted me to do. I waited. I stalled. I questioned God. I questioned myself for weeks. But, as much as I hated to admit it. I already knew the answer to my doubts and my questions. The answer was Matthew 10:33: "But whoever disowns me before others, I will disown before my Father in Heaven." So, after some additional foot dragging, I finally decided, that this was what God wanted me to do, and what I had to do. Which leads me to this book with my real name on it.

I'm sure; many of you are asking, "Really, why you? And why Donald J. Trump?" I'm sure others are saying, "You really expect us to believe that God gets involved in politics? And that God is going to choose Donald Trump over Hillary Clinton! Pleeseeee!" Believe me when I say, I know where you are coming from. I had the same struggle myself. I never did find out the answer as to why me. Why does God pick certain people for certain tasks? I cannot answer that. But, I know he does. Perhaps, it was because both political parties, the political experts, analysts, and newscasters, think that people like me could not and will not VOTE for Donald Trump. To be truthful, typically, in a typical election year, and if I had not heard God speak to me; they would be right.

According to a large majority of, come to find out, very biased newscasters and political opponents, he's rude. He's not politically correct, he says whatever is on his mind. He doesn't play political games. He doesn't have a party of speech writers who analyzes everything, he says, BEFORE he says it. (Even though sometimes I wish he did.) He doesn't pour over the polls, thinking how can I get this group of people or that group to vote for me. And we all know; he certainly doesn't target spin or try to 'soft peddle' anything. He doesn't spend hours thinking, what do I need to say to convince them I their guy? What spin can I give them? How can I twist what I mean and aim it right at them, so I can get their vote? Because, after all, with most politicians, as we have all come to know, it's the spin that matters. As I have sadly come to realize through my journey into the world of politics, most politicians only care about a person's vote. After the election, they do what their donors want. It's a game about money, the polls, the votes, and getting elected. It's not about saying what they really mean, or addressing the real issues in America, with straight talk. Heck, a lot of the real issues in America we are not supposed to talk about. If we did, we might insult someone, or be politically incorrect. We have a lot of elephants in this country, and for years they have just been there, sitting and fuming in the background, and getting larger and larger.

Donald Trump and Bernie Sanders were the ONLY ONES willing to talk about the ELEPHANTS sitting in plain sight. However, of the two, Donald Trump was the only one who was NOT a politician, and somehow I knew this was going to be important this time around. Whether we like it or not, Bernie Sanders is a politician through and through. He knows the drill. He knows the game. He has been a politician for years, and in the end, his adopted political party, for this election was the Democratic party. He was an Independent from 1979-2015. He hammered the Democrats hard on the issues. He hammered Hillary Clinton; but at the end of the day, he bargained and made a deal, to get some of his issues on the party platform. A platform which goes nowhere outside of the convention. Which just went to show me even more, the depths of our country being ruled by a very select, few individuals, party leaders, and wealthy backers. Whether we want to admit it or not, we have become a plutocracy/oligarchy. We favor the rich, and give power to the political elite, who does their bidding. In the end, unfortunately, Bernie showed us that he is just another politician, and just another spin doctor. For the remainder of this election, he will tell the American voters, and his supporters, that the issues he campaigned on, and the issues he fought hard are on, can be solved by the one person he campaigned viciously against. Even though the Clintons have abused the system, and are the poster children for the everything he rallied against. In the end, unfortunately, in my opinion, he sold out. Whereas, Donald Trump is still standing, even though he started in a field of 17, and even though several Old-Guard Republicans have turned against him. And, even though the Never Trumpers, are trying once again, to take away votes from Trump, and give Hillary the edge. Trump, against all odds, against a press that attacks him daily, against the large and well-funded and organized DNC, won the Republican party nomination, and still stands up and says it like he sees it.

I do agree that at times, Donald Trump, *very, very,* bluntly says what he believes and what's on his mind, and sometimes his bluntness, messes up what he really means. What we must recognize, is that by doing so, he allows us to talk about the un-talkable. He talks about the issues that real people are talking about, whispering about, and wondering about, behind closed doors. He knows, what the majority of politicians do not. He knows that a lot of people in America are just like me. We are not stupid. We are tired of all the games politicians play to keep themselves employed in a job. A job that gives them a huge paycheck, excellent health care, and a fantastic retirement. The main thing they have to remember, is to put their own political ambitions, their party, and their financial backers, ahead of the people of United States of America.

I know because of this election process, that there are other people, like me, who are now onto the political power games and lies, and are very tired of it. I know that just like me, there are scores of people who are tired of the money games politicians are playing with the very future of our country.

As I thought about it, Donald Trump's ability to speak and talk about hard issues, and hard choices, was because God made him fearless. He gave him a loud voice, and a boisterous personality, so that he could stand out among the crowd, and be the last man standing in an original field of 17. He designed him to be the last man standing that held to his convictions, and didn't give into political correctness or power. If you remember, the Republican party was against Donald Trump. The Republican party did not want to accept the changes that Donald Trump was proposing needed to happen in

Washington. They felt he wasn't Republican enough. There are still old-guard Republicans, who are refusing to endorse Donald Trump, like the Bush family, Mitt Romney, Ted Cruz, Never Trumpers, and others. There are still Republicans who don't want to accept that the Republican party needs to change. People who don't want to recognize that the new people coming into the party are changing it. It took a long time, but Paul Ryan in his speech at the RNC, finally acknowledged this. He stated that they could be the party of change, or they could hold onto their old ways and not be the party that propels the country forward. What the American people need to realize is that the RNC, Paul Ryan and the Republican Party are the only political party in America today that is actually listening to the voices of the majority of its members. And even though some members (70 at last count) are calling for the RNC to dump Trump. They are not. The Republican Party, unlike the DNC, is not trying to subjugate the will of the people for their own purposes. They should be loudly applauded and recognized for that.

When the Democrats try to demonize Donald Trump through demonizing the Republican Party, and the financial crises that started with President Clinton and came to fruition under President Bush, you have to remember that Donald Trump is not even being supported by President Bush. Donald Trump is not advocating President Bush type changes. He is running to bring change to the country as a whole, and to try to take money out of politics.

Ask yourself this question: 'Are you, a Republican or a Democrat, or are you an AMERICAN first? In the political world of Washington being a strict Republican or strict Democrat - before being an American - has divided America. Ideological rigidity has brought America to the terrible impasse it is at today. We vote for people to go to Congress to solve America's problems by working together and finding some common ground. Instead, the *public servants* we send to Washington are too busy bending to the far right or the far left, and will not budge. This is not serving America; this is ruining America. And it is ruining our political process. Recently, a number of Never Trump Republicans, ex-politicians, and current elected officials have come out and said they cannot vote for Donald Trump because of his rhetoric. But, I would challenge them to look beyond the words at each candidates' actions. Actions speak louder than words.

They need to reevaluate, in my opinion, in light of the $400 million in cash secretly given to Iran. In light of the millions upon millions of dollars given to the Clinton's personally, and the $2 billion given to their foundation. In light of the many statements Hillary Clinton has made, that the press and others have proven outright were incorrect and really not truthful. I hope they do. But I don't know; many are the same people who themselves, are caught up in the political mire of present day politics. They are either the rich, or the benefiters of the rich. They may have decided that it is better to let the side that knows the inner workings and old-guard way of doing things (Democrats) win, vs. have to come clean for the American people.

I have listened, night after night, to the majority of political analysts talk about how terrible it is that the majority of the Republican voters, and young voters, are so angry. They theorize that their frustration and anger are fueling Donald Trump's and Bernie Sander's rise. They go on to say how terrible it will be for our country if we allow our anger and frustration to push us to change, and push Donald Trump or Bernie Sanders into the White House.

To this end, the Democratic National Committee, a committee that is supposed to be totally impartial to all their candidates during the primaries, and let the voters have their say by picking the nominee of the party, decided that they would do whatever was needed to torpedo Bernie Sanders' campaign; thus, allowing Hillary Clinton to win the primary. Therefore, during the primaries, the DNC purposely did a variety of things, aimed at harming Bernie Sanders' campaign. I am not making this up; you can read about it by googling: hacked DNC emails. This shows all you need to know about the DNC. It will also show you how they made fun of a black American for her name; how they sold off admittance to events for money; allowed wealthy people to 'buy' presidential appointments based, sometimes on being the highest donor, etc. Even to the point of deciding who gets to sit where! The more money you donated to DNC, the closer the donor got to sit to the

President, Secretary Clinton, or wherever, by whomever, you want to sit.

It's true that's anger can be used for good or evil. When it comes to America, it appears that the Democratic party and the old-guard Republicans, forgot that it was angry colonists that pushed for the Revolutionary War that started our country. It was anger over slavery that caused the Civil War. It was anger that led us to victory in World War II. It was anger that fueled the Civil Rights Movement. It was anger that caused us to go after Osama bin Laden and al-Qaeda after the attacks on 9/11. And it may just be that same anger that forces change in America in 2016.

In the fourth-century BC, the citizens of Athens had the same type of fight that we are having in America today. They had to restore their country to a democracy from oligarchical coups. Once restored they came up with a method of drawing lots to select their government officials. They were hoping this method would prevent the formations of a 'professional governing class' (sound familiar – that is exactly what we have now) that would end up using their skills for their own benefit, as had happened in the past.

Our forefather's thought by having three separate branches of government this wouldn't happen to us. But it has. It is natural; I suppose. Once a person gets in a position, they invest so much of themselves into that position, that they don't want to lose it. Then along comes big money, wining and dining by lobbyists, the power of the position itself, and you are ripe for oligarchy. I'm sure, our current group of politicians will say, 'Not true!' We are not, in any way, shape, or form, an oligarchy! Well, let's look at the definition of oligarchy compliments of Wikipedia:

> 'Oligarchy, from Greek meaning "to rule or to command," is a form of power structure in which power effectively rests with a small number of people. These people might be distinguished by royalty, wealth, family ties, educations, corporate, religious, or military control. Such states are often controlled by a few prominent families who typically pass their influence from one generation to the next, but inheritance is not a necessary condition for the application of this term.'

Some people use the word plutocracy to define the America of today. Here is the definition of plutocracy, also compliments of Wikipedia:

> Plutocracy, from the Greek words' ploutos meaning "wealth," and kratos meaning "power." It is a form of oligarchy and defines a society ruled or controlled by the small minority of the wealthiest citizens.'

As Bernie Sanders and Donald Trump, stated over and over during the primaries, America is controlled by the elite, by a few very rich and powerful people and career politicians (professional governing class), who have rigged the system in their favor. For the rest of America, the deck is stacked against us. I believe that each of Bernie Sanders supporters, who also believe this, needs to ask themselves, why I am now supporting the very person who, along with her husband are in the top 1% of all Americans? A person who represents, and has represented for years, the top 1% of America – Hillary Clinton?

America was founded on the principle that WE the people, notice the main word, here is WE, not they or you, but WE - the people govern our country. It was not about one group overpowering another. It was about all groups coming together. That is not happening right now, and will not – unless, a person who cannot be bought is voted into office. A person who does not think that compromise or making a deal is a dirty word, a person who has brought people together before to reach a common goal. Where reaching the goal, having a vision as a country, has greater value and purpose that in-fighting and territorial posturing.

I believe this is why; God gave us an outsider. Both sides, Democratic and Republican, has shown they will not respect or listen to someone from the 'other side.' We need a person who is willing to be a moderate on some positions, such as health care. A person who says, ok I can give here on this, but this other part is non-negotiable. So that both sides feel that at the end of the day, they have won something. Right now, it's just about one side defying the other; it's about one side pushing its will on the other. Because they know that the only way, they can stay in office (the ultimate goal) is by unconditionally doing the will of their financial backers. We need a person with a big mouth, who is willing to speak up when, and if, both sides refuse to budge.

I have come to see through this election process, that the American voters are not stupid. I believe that the majority of Americans realize that we live in a complex country with vying viewpoints, goals, aspirations, beliefs, desires, backgrounds, hurts, disappointments, cultures, and histories. I think that the majority of Americans understand that we will not always agree. That we may argue. That we may verbally fight, but at the end of the day; no matter who we are, where we come from, what the color of our skin is, what religious views we hold – we are Americans. We want our country to thrive. We want our country's leaders to fight for us, to put us first, to look out for our best interests. We know that a strong America, economically strong, militarily strong, border strong, drug-free strong, family strong, governmentally strong, is a country in which we can **all** prosper and thrive. Donald Trump gets this too. He also understands that it will never, ever, happen as long as money stays in politics and the politicians are beholden to their wealthy donors.

I have also come to realize, that a country where one section or another is disenfranchised from the process is not a strong America. And throughout this election process, I have realized that Donald Trump understands this as well. All of us have to rise up, not just some. When you listen to Donald Trump talk, he is not talking about just jobs for the rich, just jobs for the elite, just jobs for the college educated. He is talking about jobs for **all** Americans, of all colors, of all backgrounds, and of all nationalities. He is talking about an economy that works for all Americans.

When Hillary Clinton was running for Senator of New York, during her campaign, she stated that she was going to create 200,000 jobs in an area that was hit especially hard by the loss of manufacturing jobs. She did not. According to an article in The Washington Post, dated August 7, 2016, written by Jerry Markon, her "efforts fell flat." She stated that she would inspire, "...the biggest investment in new, good-paying jobs since World War II." Her husband, ex-President Bill Clinton, recently stated when on the campaign trail, that she became the region's "de facto economic development officer." Well, after having eight years to create jobs, manufacturing jobs plunged by 25%, and her promised jobs – of any type - didn't happen. Umm, excuse me, can we please have a new "de facto economic development officer?"

The article, also mentioned, that in typical Clinton fashion, what Hillary did promote and get funding for, was "pet" projects involving those who financially were loyal to the Clintons. The press has actually given it a name, "pay-to-play." The Clinton's are world-wide masters at the game. The article went on to talk about how Clinton has supported e-Bay. In return, eBay's then CEO, John Donahoe, whose wife who worked for Clinton at the State Department, held a fundraiser for her in 2015. That same year, eBay paid Clinton $315,000 for a 20-minute speech. That comes to $15,750 a minute! More than some people make in a year. What could she possibly say that would be worth $15,750 a minute? In addition, eBay's charitable foundation gave $50,000 to the Clinton's foundation? (The same foundation that pays Chelsea Clinton $1,000,000/year.) This is an excellent article; I highly encourage everyone to read it. It really will give you insight into the world of inner-connected politics, money, and power. You can find it by Googling: Washington Post, Clinton, 200,000 jobs, article by Jerry Markon.

Hillary Clinton has talked for years about equal pay for women, as Chelsea did at the DNC. During a recent, Facebook Live event; Chelsea was asked what she would say to Ivanka Trump about how she would influence her father on this issue, when he hasn't addressed it yet on the campaign trail. If I was Ivanka, I would have answered by saying, "Chelsea, there is a huge difference between actions and words. My father, and the entire Trump organization, have lived it. We have hired women and promoted them to top leadership positions. I would ask you to look at your own foundation. Why are you not living it? Why are you paying women less and hiring more men than women in the top leadership positions, in the one company you can control?"

The one thing we can all control is our own lives. If we have companies, organizations, or foundations that are ours, then the best place to start is there with actions that support our beliefs. We can live what we say and what we believe. According to an article by The Daily Caller News Foundation, titled *Exclusive Pay Gap Alert: Clinton Foundation Male Execs Earn 38% More Than Women;* by Richard Pollock dated 4/12/2016, the Clinton family are not living what they say they believe, in regard to, their own family foundation. A foundation where they call all the shots. The Clintons have the ability to hire whom they want, pay what they want, for all foundation employees, yet, they have chosen to pay women less. In regard to their top management, it was found that men far outnumber women. Men are paid on average $109,000 **more** than women. Why is this? Because there are no viable women out there to hire? Because only men are qualified for the top positions? The question I would like to ask Chelsea and Hillary is, "When are they going to start acting on your own belief of equal pay/equal opportunity for women? Don't you think that using your own foundation, as an example, would be an excellent place to start?"

When we listen to politicians talk about the issues, we have to remember that they are fishing for our votes.

Sorry Hillary! God Wants Trump!

The article mentioned above, by Jerry Markon, talks about this as well. Politicians, like Hillary Clinton, are excellent at knowing what to say, but if we want to see what they really believe, we need to see how they live.

Why America Needs Trump

Now More Than Ever
America Needs a
Businessman

As mentioned earlier, Donald Trump is the only person running who has not been in politics before. He is the only person running who was self-funded during the primaries. He did not take money from special-interest groups or Super PACS. This is huge. He is the ultimate outsider.

On the issue of campaign-finance reform, corruption, and control of our very political process by the wealthy, Bernie Sanders and Donald Trump agree. It must change, and it must change now. Bernie Sanders has admitted that to make such a change will not be easy. It will take compromise and the total backing of the American people to make our elected officials do what needs to be done for these laws to change. It will require new laws, the overturning of a Supreme Court decision, and for the legislators to give up all the money and perks that special-interest groups provide, not an easy task. In addition, it will require politicians to end the back scratching, favoritism, and pay-to-play mentality mastered by the Clintons.

During the primary, Donald Trump did none of this. He just did it the old-fashioned way. He basically said, 'No thanks, I don't need your money. I'll just self-fund my campaign, for as long as I can.' I know that as he now goes through the general election process, he will still be his own person; even though he needs to generate millions of dollars in donations just to even compete against the Clinton money machine. That is just who he is. He knows how the system works, and he will not be beholden to anyone, money or no money. Which I'm sure is driving a lot of ultra-rich people and the professional governing class up the wall. I'm sure they are saying, "I mean, who does he think he is? Who in the heck do *his voters* think they are? We decide and only we decide what and how our government operates. We don't listen to the people. We listen to donors, the lobbyists, and special interest groups with money. You rub my back, and I'll rub yours. That's the way we roll around here."

They have totally discounted the impact of Donald Trump and his supporters. Donald Trump's and Bernie Sanders' supporters have figured out the game, and they don't like it. They want change. They want an outsider. They, like I have come to understand, don't want the rich and powerful and the professional ruling class controlling our country anymore. This is exactly why I believe that Donald Trump is the only person for the job.

President Obama recently said that he did not believe Donald Trump would ever be President. President Obama said being President is tougher than being on reality TV, and he believed that the American people were too "sensible" to elect him. I hope he is wrong. I hope we, the American people, take back our country, and realize voting for Trump is the only sensible thing to do! President Obama apparently forgot that Donald Trump has done a lot of things, other than appear on television. He has created a multi-billion-dollar real estate empire made up of hotels and golf courses around the world. He created the Trump brand, which is recognized all over the world for being a sign of excellence and quality. He created thousands upon thousands of jobs. According to a CNN, he created anywhere from 34,000 to 67,000 jobs. He has dealt with countries and governments from around the world. He created his own modeling agency. He restored the famous Wollman Skating Rink in Central Park, after a seven-year effort by the city. He took over and completed it in four months for less than one-tenth of the projected cost, with his own money! Think about that for a moment. It cost him one-tenth of the projected cost and four months, not the 84 months the city already took, and failed to complete it in. He has authored, or co-authored with ghost writers, 15 books to date, all of which have been best-sellers. He is one of the highest paid speakers in the world. He has held WWE wrestling events. And the list goes on and on. This is not a person who just acts in a reality TV show. This is a person of substance who has created a real estate and business brand and empire here in the U.S. and around the world. This didn't happen by accident. This took levelheadedness, dedication, planning, knowledge, innovation, creatively, competitiveness, judgement, and **leadership**.

I believe that God made Donald Trump a tough talker. He speaks him mind, sometimes in a rather colorful way. He doesn't try to be politically correct, but he tries to get the real issues out on the table. Donald Trump said we should ban Muslims from entering our country **UNTIL** we are able to determine and understand the problem and the dangerous threat it could potentially pose by unknowingly allowing jihadists and radical Islamic terrorists to enter. Our country cannot be the victims of horrendous attacks by people that believe in jihad, and have no sense of reason, or respect for human life. The press went wild. The Democratic party went wild. Some Muslims went wild. Accusations were, once again, made that Donald Trump was a racist, etc. But did you notice, he said **only until** we can figure out what is going on. Doesn't it make you wonder how inept Hillary Clinton and company, and the media, think our Homeland Security, and governmental personnel are, if they believe that banning Muslims would be a forever deal? They must be assuming that they would never get it figured out, and therefore, Muslims would never be allowed to enter the United States again. Donald Trump's point was, how are people who believe in jihad and are radical Islamic terrorists, whose only goal is to destroy us, getting into our country?

I find it interesting, that it was only **after Trump** brought this issue up, we found out; well by golly, ISIS has confiscated real, honest, to goodness, passport machines, capable of making fake passports and identities, which are exactly like the real ones! Say, "What?" Why wasn't this mentioned before? This was known for months. Yet, this grave risk was kept from the American public, until Donald

Trump brought up the issue. We need to know the issues. We need a President who is not afraid to say what they are. A President who is not afraid to say, this is a risk. We've got to figure this out. How can we keep America and Americans safe, while at the same time finding out who the jihadists are that are entering the U.S. with real looking, but actually fake passports? We need to get a plan in place, and we need to do it quickly. That is common sense leadership to me.

During World War II, our President and elected officials told the American people the risks we faced if we and our allies did not win the war. This is the reason that people sacrificed, bought bonds, paid their taxes, went on rations, had victory gardens, etc. Americans were brought into the process, not left out of it.

However, in our current fight against ISIS, it has been reported that under President Obama, the White House wanted it reported that we were winning the war on ISIS; therefore, the intelligence reports were changed – after they were originally written, to reflect this. It became so bad, that 50 intelligence analysts working for the U.S. Military's Central Command **formally** complained that their reports were being "inappropriately altered by senior officials." That is unbelievable. Do you realize the guts it took for them to do that? They should be recognized as American heroes. The military is all about chain-of-command and never making anyone above them look bad.

However, some of CENTCOM's top officials, who were the ones briefing the President, changed the reports to reflect the narrative that Obama, and the White House wanted to give the American people; which was that we were winning the war on terror when, in reality the reports said we were not. Changing the reports before they got to President Obama and the White House press office, gave the President and his staff, plausible deniability, in case it ever came out. I think they were afraid of getting political backlash if the real truth came out. In addition, it would have shown that what we are currently doing is not working, and would have supported the call for change in the White House. To read more about this, please go to: thedailybeast.com. Look up the report written by Shane Harris and Nancy A. Yourself dated 09.09.15 titled 'Cancer Within:' Exclusive: 50 Spies Say ISIS Intelligence Was Cooked.

We all know that as President, Donald Trump, would want to see the real reports as originally written, warts and all. And, I believe he would tell us the truth about them. Like he recently did, in Maine, he talked about the current conditions in the country of Somalia. And how dangerous it is there. He was attacked for doing so, because a large number of Muslim refugees have come to the United States from Somalia. So, I looked it up. Did he lie about it? No. Did he state things that were not true? No. Did he attack the refugees living here in the U.S. from Somalia? No. He only spoke the truth to the voters of Bangor Maine, about the conditions in Somalia today. A large number of ISIS terrorists are going there and hoping to spread out from there to the West. But see, we aren't supposed to talk about this, because it might make someone who fled that country and came to America look bad by association. Wait. They fled there; they were refugees, and now talking about the very dangers they fled, is bad? It appears, in our hyper-sensitive, politically correct world of today, we can't talk about what is going on in a country, somewhere in the world today, because it might make someone who fled that country look bad! I don't understand this thinking at all. He is not making up what is going on there. He did not attack the people who came from there to the U.S. He talked about the risks associated with that country today, because of ISIS. For this, he was attacked and called, and I quote, "racist, fascist, slime..." What he said was, ".... Somali refugees (are) coming from among the most dangerous territories or countries in the world." True statement. I'm sorry if refugees from Somalia find this comment offense. If it's not true, why did they flee there?

Donald Trump has spoken up about trade deals with China, about the terrible deal made with Iran (the greatest terrorist sponsor on the face of this earth) that gave them not only $400,000,000 in cash, but $1.3 billion more as an interest payment. The money did nothing, in my humble opinion, because after we gave Iran the cash and paid them $1.3 billion in interest, Iran's supreme leader, Ayatollah Ali Khamenei, said, the United States is "worse than all terrorists." He went on to say that the "US cannot be trusted." Then Iran preceded to arrest and hold three new American hostages.

Donald Trump has spoken out about how he feels that a lot of the deals the U.S. has made with other countries have weakened America. The negotiators gave more to the other countries than they did to the USA. He has spoken up about how they were basically unfair deals, that favored the other side, instead of being of equal benefit to both parties. He is not the only one saying this, Bernie Sanders said the same thing. But, he is the only one still in the race, with the guts to say it out loud to the American people, all across the country. If you were going to send someone to negotiate with Iran and China, who do you think has bluntness, tenancy, and ability to do so effective? I say Donald Trump, because God made him this way.

I have heard a political analyst say, 'Doesn't Trump get it; Presidents don't negotiate with other countries. That is what diplomats do.' Well, it may have been done that way in the past, but I believe if the President of the United States determines that the negotiations are very important to the country as a whole, and wants to do it, I'm pretty darn sure there is no law stopping him.

Donald Trump has spoken on taking care of our vets. He knows that the real cost of the war is far greater than the cost of military spending. It is the cost of the lives of the soldiers who are asked to fight for our country. It is the cost of rehabilitation for soldiers injured while fighting, the cost of treating PTSD, the cost of soldiers living without limbs, living without hope, the cost of soldiers returning addicted to drugs, and the list could go on and on. Did you notice that Donald Trump was the only Presidential candidate to mention tackling the massive fraud issues at the Department of Veteran Affairs? This is just one of the many ways needed to ensure our vets are taken care of by making the most of every dollar and not allowing money allocated for vets to be stolen from them.

Let's get one thing straight; unlike Hillary Clinton, Donald Trump is not running for President in order to increase his own wealth. Bill and Hillary personally, and The Bill, Hillary & Chelsea Clinton Foundation raked in millions upon millions of dollars; including $2 billion to date for their foundation, from governments, dictators, and business around the world. All of this has been since Bill Clinton left the White House, including while Hillary Clinton was a Senator for New York, and while she was Secretary of State. Just think of what can happen if she becomes President. In addition, to what they have personally received, what their foundation has received, supporters of Bill and Hillary are also investing money with their son-in-law's investment company, called Eaglevale Partners. The fund currently manages $330 million dollars, and new investors have to give them $2 million, if they want to be a client. This appears to me, to just be another access point for the rich and wealthy.

I'm not saying his company has done anything inappropriate or illegal. However, others have made accusations that he got inside information during the time his mother-in-law was Secretary of State. Maybe it was just from dinner time conversations about the state of the world. Who knows? It is my understanding that his company tries to invest and make money from instabilities and regime changes around the world, like Greece. Wow! I never even knew that investment companies even thought of investing in another country's economic woes. I think Andrew Stiles, editor of the Washington Free Beacon, had an interesting take on it. In an editor's blog, dated Feb. 4, 2015, he stated, after Eaglevale lost 90% of its investors' money betting on Greece, "This is not to say that giving your money to Eaglevale is a bad investment. Of course, if your primary concern is short-term profit, you should probably look elsewhere. But if you are a wealthy democratic donor who places a high value on long-term political access to one of America's most powerful families, Eaglevale is the fund for you. Not surprisingly, the fund's early group sessions for prospective investors attracted "stand-room-only crowds." He continued by noting, "Prominent investors include Lloyd Blankfein, chairman and CEO of Goldman Sachs, where Mezvinsky used to work. Blankfein has contributed generously to Democrats over the years, and has hosted fundraisers for Hillary Clinton." He went on, "Marc Lasry, the billionaire hedge fund manager who co-owns the Milwaukee Bucks, is also an investor. Lasry, who used to employ Chelsea Clinton at his $13.3 billion hedge fund, Avenue Capital Group, is a longtime democratic donor and figures to be one of Hillary Clinton's top fundraisers in 2016. Lasry had been President Obama's choice to serve as U.S. ambassador to France, but was forced to withdraw his name over his ties to an alleged poker ring run by the Russian mob." (What?? Did I just read that right? I had to double check, yep a guy associated with the Russian mob is one of Hillary Clinton's top fundraiser. WOW!) He ended with, "Wall Street tycoons are clearly ready for Hillary, and there are few better ways to show that than by giving money to her son-in-law to play with. He might not be any good at it, but he does know someone who might live in the White House one day. And that's where the real money gets made." I'll just let you take a moment and let all of this sink in...

The Clintons are the first United States governmental officials to go around the world collecting mass amounts of money for themselves from foreign multi-national companies, governments, and dictatorships. Peter Schweizer wrote a book about it called 'Clinton Cash: The Untold Story of How and Why Foreign Governments and Businesses Helped Make Bill and Hillary Rich.'

In addition to the above, it came out on August 1, 2016 that Hillary Clinton took $100,000 from a company in

France, Lefarge, that had paid money to ISIS to operate its cement plant in Syria. In addition, Lefarge, bought oil from ISIS for years. In the early 1990s and 1980s when Hillary was connected to Lefarge, the firm was implicated in facilitating a CIA-backed covert arms' export network to Saddam Hussein. Remember Saddam Hussein, the evil of the world that we had to take out? We thought he had nuclear weapons, but then found out, after the invasion and searching the entire country – oops, our bad. He didn't! Sorry, Iraq. Oh, yea we can't say, sorry yet, we're still there. To read more about Hillary's Lefarge dealings go to the gatewaypundit.com and look up *WIKILEAKS: Hillary took cash from Company Accused of Sponsoring ISIS* written by Jim Hoft dated August, 1, 2016.

In 2011, Secretary of State Hillary Clinton, accused the Moroccan government of "arbitrary arrest and corruption in all branches of government." In 2014, they gave her foundation $1 million to host a conference, and she praised them for being "a vital hub for economic and cultural exchange." Lol! Isn't it interesting what a difference a million-dollar makes. Enemy or friend, well it depends, "Got money?"

While Hillary Clinton was Secretary of State, she worked with the Russians. Remember, who she just accused of tampering with the U.S. election and accused Donald Trump of doing business with, even though he doesn't? Well, Secretary Clinton and a number of firms from Silicon Valley worked with (our supposed enemy) Russia, to develop biomed, space, NUCLEAR, and IT technologies in a program called "Skolkovo." It appears, that several of the firms involved gave tens of millions to the Clinton's Foundation, to Bill Clinton for speeches, and to companies with 'deep ties to the Clinton's.' (Tens of Millions!) This project did not reset our relations with Russia, and some very viable security experts fear it put the United States at grave risk for the future security of our country. In the end, it looks like, the only American people, who really made out from this endeavor were the Clintons. Russia made out quite well too. The FBI feared the Russia's real motive was "to gain access to our classified, sensitive, and emerging technology," per a memo sent out by Lucia Ziobro, assistant special agent to the FBI. Russia, soon after this joint endeavor, was able to develop hypersonic cruise-missile engines, radar surveillance equipment, and vehicles capable of delivering airborne Russian troops, per the below listed article in the Wall Street Journal. Yeah! Secretary Clinton! Yeah Russia! I feel so safe now! You can read about it in the New York Post. Google: *Report raises questions about 'Clinton Cash' from Russians during 'reset'* by Laura Italiano dated July 31, 2016. Also, read The Wall Street Journal, commentary by Peter Schweizer, dated July 31, 2016, titled *The Clinton Foundation, State and Kremlin Connections.*

Here is the interesting thing about the Clintons, in 2001 when President Clinton and Hillary left the White

House, they have stated that they were $8 million in debt. They were able to make a positive change of $12 million in one year, making them worth $4 million by the end of the year. As stated, they did this by giving speeches around the world to large companies, governments, and dictatorships. As of 2016, Hillary Clinton was worth $31.3 million and Bill Clinton was worth $80 million. Total $111 million.

Hillary Clinton does not own any real estate or have any debt. Which means her money must be in stocks, cash, or governmental bonds. From January 2009 to Feb. 2013 when she was Secretary of State, she earned $186,800 per year. When she was in the Senate, from Jan. 2001 to Jan. 2009, she made $174,000 per year. In twelve years, she was able to recover from $4 million dollars' worth of debt (her half of the $8 million.) AND save enough money to buy between $5 million and $20 million in money-market funds, stocks, bonds, etc. All while working as a public servant. Wow! This does not even begin to count Bill Clinton's earnings.

How could she have done this? I don't know. Let's take a closer look. Let's just assume that Bill paid off the $8 million in debt along with all the family bills, so that she was able to just invest all of her earnings, after taxes. Let's assume, she paid a 30% tax rate. At $174,000/year that would have left her, after taxes with $121,800 per year, for the eight years she was a Senator. Her cumulative total earnings for those eight years would have been $974,400.

As Secretary of State she was earning $186,800 per year, net after 30% taxes would have been $130,760. At the end of those four years she would have had $523,040. If she saved all her money, during that twelve-year period, she would have earned almost $1.5 million after taxes. If she had started investing in 2001 the S&P 500 lost 11.85% that year, and it lost another 21.97% in 2002. Then made money from 2003-2007, before losing 36.55% in 2008. The S&P 500 grew 59.93% from 2009-2012. The overall average return from 2001-2012 for the S&P 500 average return was 4.5%. During this 12-year period a typical investor would have seen an investment of $1.5 million grow to a little more than $2 million. Hillary was able to turn $121,000-$130,00/year or $1,500,000 cumulative in somewhere between $5 million -$26 million! That is three to 17 times more than the average investor would have earned during that same time period. Remember that the 2008 bear marker was so severe that it took most investor till 2012 just to get back to even. I guess the one thing we can say about Hillary is, she is lucky! Not only did she get back to even, she surpassed it, in amazing fashion. Can I please have Hillary's investment team? Please!

Before Bill Clinton became President, their combined net worth was only $700,000, now their combined net worth is $111 million. This is from two powerful people, who started a foundation to go around the world and do good. Amazing. You can only imagine what their net worth will be by the time Hillary Clinton leaves the White House.

Right now, Hillary is trying to portray Russia as our enemy, because Putin has been flattering of Donald Trump, but remember Skolkovo and Operation Russia Reset? Or Morocco? I have a feeling that after a few million dollars in donations from Russia to the Clinton's Foundation, or to Bill or Hillary for speaking fees, that could change. After all, don't forget that one of her top campaign fundraisers has ties to a Russian mob.

Jimmy Carter has been going around the world with his Carter Center for 25 years, waging peace, fighting diseases, and building hope. Yet, he is only worth $5 million; which he earned from writing books. Too bad he didn't understand the financial power of his position. Instead of donating money to these countries, he obviously should have been giving speeches and asking them for money. Isn't that what we have now learned from the Clintons?

Donald Trump, on the other hand, does not need the job or the money. God gave us a candidate who is financially independent. He is running for the right reason, because he believes that our country is headed in the wrong direction. He knows that he has the skill set, and a life time of experiences, that will enable him to help get our country on the right path once again. He realized, that during the primary, it was going to take a person who used their own money to run their campaign so that he won't be indebted to special interests and people looking for handouts and favors. Donald Trump will be a President for the people of our country, the citizens who call America home, not special interests, the ultra-wealthy, or career politicians (the professional governing class), like the Clintons, who were able to capitalize on their positions to increase their own wealth.

What politicians don't understand about Donald Trump is that he is a leader, even though, he at times, speaks a little too bluntly. I'm not the only one saying this. Surprisingly, even John McCain recently said so. Right now, Trump's opponents are saying, 'Tell us how you're going to do these things, and we will then analyze it, and see if we agree.' Which in political language means 'so we will tear it to smithereens.' I believe, this is not what real leaders do. Leaders say, this is the goal. Then they get everybody on board to achieve that goal. For example, Trump says, 'I'm going to bring jobs back to America. I'm going to talk to the CEO of American companies and see what we can do together to make it happen'. He also recognizes that this will take the involvement and support of the Senate, the House, various companies, and the American people. He recognizes, and has said, he will need the cooperation of Congress because laws will have to be passed making it more business friendly and desirable for these companies to return to America. Currency issues between the U.S.,

China and other countries, will need to be addressed, and so on. Donald Trump knows the process that needs to happen. He will work hard to make it happen. The one thing that makes Donald Trump not quit, is being told it can't be done. He loves a challenge, and as a country right now, we have plenty of them. He will not just sit back and say, well sorry folks, it's not happening. He will work night and day to change the minds and hearts of Congress to make it happen for the American people. And, you know; we may have to help out a little too, by putting pressure on our elected officials to put down their swords and work together with the President on all of these important issues. I'm sure a writing campaign, an e-mail campaign, a twitter campaign, and an old-fashion phone campaign, from millions of voters to Congress will get our point across.

Whereas, the Democratic response is to vote in more democratic representatives so that they can win the majority of votes in both houses, and not need to deal with the Republican party. The ultimate test will be if the 'professional governing class' works towards real change in America, or if only by voting out all sitting politicians can, we the people, get our country back. Time will tell.

But even in light of this, Donald Trump knows that reaching a compromise it not going to be easy. It takes work, hard work, but necessary work. He is a goal-oriented person. He is a hard, hard worker. When it was recently mentioned that he had not had to make any sacrifices to this country. He stated that he felt he had, because he had worked very, very hard to be successful and to be able to provide jobs for thousands of people. He was kind of scoffed at for this answer. But, I think he did recognize that with great wealth, comes great responsibility. And to keep his employees and his family members employed, he had to keep working and expanding his company. He has stated before that he believes his first two marriages ended in divorce because he was a workaholic.

This is not meant to be in any way, disrespectful or ungrateful to Khizr and Ghazala Khan. The loss of their son, Humayun Khan at the age of 27 from a car bomb in Iraq in 2004, is every parents' worst nightmare. Their son did pay the ultimate sacrifice. And my heart goes out to them. I think it is absolutely a sad thing, that we even got involved in the Iraq War, that we are still involved in the Iraq War, and that due to this war, we have lost so many outstanding children, fathers, daughters, and sons, like the Khan's son. To date, the Iraq war has not made the world a safer place. In fact, it has become less safe because of it. I do believe that, in America, the Khan's have the right to question, and state their opinion of, any person running for any political office. The fact that the DNC gave them a loud voice, is their right also. In addition, I could see the pain on both of their faces, and I would never expect them both to speak, or question why Ghazala Khan did not speak.

I also feel that it is not right, that Hillary Clinton, also chose to question a Gold Star mother. During the Democratic debate on March 9, 2016, Hillary Clinton said that Patricia Smith, mother of slain U.S. Foreign Service Officer Sean Smith, 'lied'. Well ok, she didn't use that word, but it meant the same thing, the words she used, was "...she's wrong. She's absolutely wrong." So, if she is absolutely wrong, then she lied?? Because Patricia Smith, over and over again, has denied that she heard what Hillary Clinton said incorrectly; and she stands by her recollection. I am sure that, all of the media and our elected officials, are just as upset about Secretary Clinton's comments about Patricia Smith. It's just that they haven't voiced it to the American people, *yet*. Secretary Clinton, said that she did not hold it against the families that during their time of grief, they did not remember what she told them. Wait, what? I guess that Secretary Clinton didn't realize that Patricia Smith is not the only one whose memory is, "faulty.'" The Gold Star father of Tyrone Woods, another Benghazi victim, remembers Hillary Clinton's comments the exact same way.

It makes me wonder, if at times of stress, as the Benghazi attack certainly was, if Hillary Clinton forgets what she says. I mean, who can fault her? She had to talk to a lot of different groups that night. And it has been reported, her explanation changed each time. I'm sure it was due to the stress of the situation. When running for President in 2008, Hillary Clinton talked about being under fire by snipers as she landed in Bosnia during a trip in 1996. Unfortunately, for her there is an actual news film of the trip, which totally discredited her story, and the many versions of it, she kept saying to try to correct what she had said (forgotten) the first time. You can read about it by googling: Hillary Clinton under sniper fire landing in Bosnia in 1996, or look up the story written by Glenn Kessler here: https://www.washingtonpost.com/news/fact-checker/wp/2016/05/23/recalling-hillary-clintons-claim-of-landing-under-sniper-fire-in-bosnia/.

It is true that Donald Trump, did not serve in the military, and has not lost a son to war. Retired President Bill Clinton and President Obama did not serve in the military either. Hillary and Chelsea Clinton, and Michelle Obama, have chosen not to serve in the military. The question about whether a person, or their family, should be required to serve in the military, as being a requirement for running for President, is one that has been asked each time we have an election. However, it is not a requirement under the Constitution for running for President.

The unfortunate thing in all of this, and that I believe has been purposely lost on the media, and perhaps the American people, is that Donald Trump, being a total outsider and not a politician, has evolved as most human beings and candidates do. Unfortunately, he has had to evolve under the intense spotlight of, what appears to me to be, a very biased media. He has refined his ban on all

Muslims, to recognize that his original, ongoing, and consistent purpose, is to keep out radical Islamist extremists and jihadist from enter the United States, not peaceful Muslims. He has come to recognize that he could do a better job of this by not saying all Muslims, in general. And instead limit it to defined territories and known concentrated areas of the world where terrorists are found in large numbers, or where we have good intelligence telling us that terrorists have infiltrated the refugee population.

I acknowledge what Mr. Khan is saying. He and his wife came from Pakistan and therefore, he feels that even under these circumstances with Donald Trump's plan, he and his family would not be allowed into this country. And his brave son would never have been allowed to serve in the military. However, that is assuming that we are totally unable to verify who is a radical and who is not. I have great faith, that we have people in our government who would do their utmost to come up with a system that would minimize the risks, and come up with a fair and just system, that allows Muslims into our country while keeping out radical Islamic extremist. However, per FBI Director James Comey, we are not there, yet. This has been Donald Trump's goal and purpose all along. Unfortunately, thousands upon thousands of people like, Mr. Khan's son, gave their lives defending this country. We must honor and respect that by figuring out, and not letting in the very people he, and so many others, died defeating. I am grateful that the Khan's choose America. I am grateful for the wonderful young man they raised. Nothing, can ever repay them, or any other parent who lost a child, in this terrible war. The only thing we can do, is honor their lives and their sacrifice, by ensuring that terrorists do not get a foothold in this country in an effort to destroy it. If terrorists, are ever able to secretly build, and set off a dirty nuclear weapon in America; make bombs to destroy our cities; or gain a foothold here – then everything all of our brave men and women have fought, were injured or died for – will have been in vain.

Ray Starman, former U.S. Army Intelligence Officer, Veteran of the Gulf War, and founder of US Defense Watch wrote a column addressed to Mr. Khan on his website US Defense Watch. It is a very insightful read. You can find it at http://www.usdefensewatch.com/2016/07/an-open-letter-to-mr-khizr-khan/. If possible, please take the time to read it.

I think it is vitally important for us to remember that, Trump was against the war in Iraq, whereas Clinton voted for it. If Trump Were President, would the Khan's have lost their son? If Trump were President, would ISIS and radical jihadist extremists, have gotten as strong as they are? We have been fighting ISIS for a little over two years. We have been fighting terrorism for almost 15 years since 9/11, but the world is less safe than when we began. Would al-Qaeda, ISIS, and other radical jihadist terrorist organizations have access to countries around the world? They now have the access and ability to continue to chop the heads off of Christians, bomb and kill citizens, kidnap individuals for ransom, and recruit new terrorists from around the world. One of the reasons they have gotten so powerful is because we did not destroy and stop their sources of income and ways of earning money early on. And now we unfortunately know, that our own President just secretly sent $400 million in cash to the one nation that supports terrorism - Iran. In addition to giving them an additional $1.3 billion in interest. (This is what we know of, remember it was only this week that we learned about the $400 million in cash, given to them in January!) President Obama said that they wanted cash because due to the sanctions, we and our allies, had placed on them, there were things they just couldn't buy, otherwise. Like what exactly? Let's see what would a country that hates our guts, hates Israel, supports terrorists, possibly want to buy with cash. Gee, I can't think of a thing, can you? Oh, wait President Obama just told us, roads and infrastructure. Yea, they are paying for roads and infrastructure with cash. Just like countries everywhere around the world do. Duh! Why didn't I think of that?

How you ever wondered what was the purpose of our sanctions to begin with? Because now it sorta feels like the parent that says, "If you don't stop breaking the rules of our house, then I will take away your allowance!" Then, the kid breaks the rules; the allowance is denied for a bit, then the parents give in, and say, "Here, sorry, let me give you more to make up for withholding your allowance." Yea, right. That really works! So cash for guns vs. cash for roads…. I don't know; it just doesn't feel right; I'm thinking guns.

Donald Trump has mentioned throughout his campaign, the absolute need to cut off all sources of money and income going to ISIS, al-Qaeda, etc. In fact, it was only after one of the Republican debates, where he hammered home this issue, that we were told that **one** of the sites were ISIS keeps its cash was bombed. That was just this year, 2016, for a war that has been going on for two years, against ISIS, and 15 years counting Iraq, al-Qaeda, etc. Donald Trump also stated that he would go in and destroy any tanks, and all military equipment, left by us or others that they might start using. In addition, he would destroy their oil refineries, etc. Yet; it took until this election cycle for us to even bomb one of their cash holding locations. Why? I think we didn't think about it for starters. And for the oil refineries, President Obama said that Iraq asked us not to destroy ISIS's oil refineries. Yea, that's a good reason! Wasn't that nice of us? Let's let them have the money, they need to fund their operations, because Iraq asked us too. Gee, we are so nice. Forget all about our soldiers who died fighting or were injured during this time, or ISIS's ability to grow, chop off heads of Christians, rape women, etc. Iraq said no, so it's no. Really? I don't think that's a good enough reason.

Remember, Hillary Clinton claims Donald Trump doesn't know very much about fighting ISIS. Really? He knew enough to say take away their sources of money and that we had a problem with our vetting process. I'm sure he doesn't know how to smuggle hundreds of millions in foreign cash on pallets, into a country supporting the very terrorists; we are fighting, in an unmarked plane. But, then again, I don't think that is a necessary requirement for being, Commander-in-Chief, do you?

I just can't stop wondering, if we had not decided to depose of the Syrian President, Bashar al-Assad, and if we had taken away their income sources, would they have gotten a strong hold there? And if not, then we wouldn't even be having the decision of who to allow, or not allow, into our country and how to verify who is a radical jihadist extremist and who is not? I cannot imagine that anyone living in America, is willing to open our doors to any radical jihadist extremists. We have unfortunately, not been very good as a country at changing people's hearts away from radicalism, once they become indoctrinated. I don't know why.

I can't believe that the men and women who served in the military, and have personally seen men and women die in combat trying to fight al Qaeda, ISIS, and all forms of jihadist terrorism, would agree to letting them come in either. The question is, how do we know? How do we identify who is and who is not a radical Islamic terrorist or a terrorist of any kind? They certainly don't wear a sign announcing it for all the world to see. We can't tell by their passports. They have infiltrated with the refugees. So how do we identify them? Even though President Obama has come out and stated we have an excellent system for vetting the refugees. FBI Director, James Comey, recently reported that we do not have the capacity to properly vet, even the 10,000 Syrian refugees' President Obama wants to come into the country this year. He stated that the problem with vetting the refugees from Syria, is the difficulty of verifying their background - due to the chaos and war in that country. This is the question that Donald Trump has raised and why he made his original statement. He wants to be certain that we can vet them properly. Yes, in the beginning he used the word, all Muslims, but since that time he has refined what he meant to identify the people he is really aiming at.

When President Obama was running for President, he made 500 campaign promises. He has had about a 45% success rate. Which I'm told is actually good. However, most of the serious ones he has not been able to accomplish, because he cannot get the Senate and the House to agree with him on his plans. Our political process has become so fractured and divided that we don't work together anymore. It has become more important for our elected officials to stand their ground, than to find solutions. This is not President Obama's fault. This is not Hillary Clinton's faults. This is not the Democrats' fault, or the Republicans' fault. This is what happens when you have a professional governing class and an oligarchy that runs a country. When oligarchy/plutocracies have been around for years and years and years, as in the United States, elected officials learn the system and work the system. And it takes a revolution to change it. Revolutions do not happen quietly. If you see the Republicans coming out and refusing to vote for Donald Trump, because he wants to talk about the elephants in the room, remember this, they too are part of the professional ruling class, and they have a vested interest in maintaining the status quo. We, as a nation, need to have valid discussions about our country, without people saying how terrible it is to even mention the subject! I believe that it's ok, for Muslims, Hispanics, and even illegal immigrants to join in the discussion, and voice their opinion. They have a right to say, "I'm part of the fabric of this country too. I was born here; my parents came; we've been here for years, and you did nothing." It's all good. Discussion is good. But to call the person leading the discussion and his supporters' racist for even saying that we have a problem and here's why; is so un-American. And for a famous actor to say, Trump supporters need to be cleansed from America, is just plain immoral! We are supposed to freely discuss our differences. Not attack, and boy are the Democrats good at attacking. The people who say they are for free speech, who honors those who say, "What do we want? Dead cops! When do we want them? Now!" Who parades them up on the stage at the DNC, and basically says they have the right to free hate speech in

America. Turn around and viscously attack Donald Trump, for talking about the elephants hiding in our nation. They have called him some of the most vile, vicious, names possible. They say talking about our problems, makes him a racist. This is appalling. So, it appears that only Democrats, and those whose votes they are courting, can have free speech in America.

I do realize that President Obama and Hillary Clinton have stated what sounds like some very noble objectives and goals, and that some people believe that their vision is the right vision for our country. I don't. As I see it, the problem is not having a vision, or having goals, or objectives. The problem is the very way our country is being controlled and run. It needs to change. Our elected officials need to change. Who controls the elected officials within our government, and who benefits from our government needs to change. Money needs to get out of politics. Both parties need to wake up and realize that a real revolution is happening in America, and we cannot go back to business as usual. We cannot go back to lined pockets, favors, special appointments in exchange for donations, etc. We cannot go back to the ultra-rich, and the old-guard political establishment, running America. We cannot go back to some politicians (ex-President Bill Clinton and Secretary-of-State Hillary Clinton) being able to go around the world collecting obscene amounts of money from dictatorships, governments, and others, many of whom suppress human rights, for delivering speeches. Collaborations such as these, devalue who we are as a nation, and as people, and they cheapen everything we stand for.

If we continue along this path, we will destroy ourselves as a country. History has shown; the change needed to take on Wall Street, take on the lobbyists, take on the kickbacks, take on the systems that favors the wealthy over average citizens, take on the massive fraud, and the media that plays spin doctor (mostly in favor of the Democratic establishment), cannot come from someone who has been working in this very system for years, no matter how good or honorable they **tell us their** intentions are. It absolutely cannot come from someone who has worked the system to line their own pockets and become extremely wealthy in the process. (This is not the American dream. Hard work and building things, is the American dream. Not taking money from questionable people and corrupt governments that deny LGBT, women, and girls equal rights.) Change can only come from an outsider. It can only come from someone who is **fearless** and willing to state what needs to be stated. It can only come as a clear mandate from the people of our country. We need an outsider in Washington, now more than ever in the history of our country. If you get nothing else out of the book, I hope you really pray about and understand this.

As mentioned previously, the best example of why things needs to change, just came from what President Obama did by secretly paying $400 million dollars in cash -

CASH to **Iran**. $400 million consisting of euros, Swiss francs, and other currencies, was stacked on pallets, put on a plane, and secretly flown to Iran. Why was in done in secret? Because U.S. law **FORBIDS** any transaction involving American dollars with Iran. Oh, and by the way, President Obama and his staff also want you to believe, that this is a totally separate thing, from the four Americans hostages who were released by Iran, at the exact same time. What are the odds of that? Remember, America doesn't pay ransoms. America is forbidden by law to give any U.S. dollars to Iran. But our very own President, found a way around our **own** law! This is oligarchy/plutocracy at its absolutely worst. I believe that this is corruption at its very worse. As much as President Obama, his White House press secretary, John Earnest, and the political press spin teams, try to tell us this was all-above-board and for our best interest, it was not. If this was something that was legal and perfectly normal to be done, then the American people and our elected officials in Congress, would have been told about this transfer of cash. If it was all-above-board and legal, it wouldn't have been paid in cash made up of foreign currency and flown secretly to Iran. It was all done under the table. Now, America, Israel, and the world, are at a far greater risk for terror attacks and American citizens are at a greater risk of being kidnapped, in Iran and around the world, than ever before.

Along with President Obama, his press secretary, John Earnest, is also telling us to just believe that it was all a coincidence, that it magically just happened to occur at the same time as the settlement of the Iran arms deal dispute. One team was negotiating for the release of hostages, and the other team negotiating a settlement for the 1979 arms deal. The hostage release negotiating team wanted the money delivered to show that the United States was making progress on reaching a deal. So, wait, they weren't talking to each other, but somehow they did talk to each other, didn't they? Those darn cell phones!

Unfortunately, since that payment to Iran, Iran has captured **three** additional Americans in an effort to get President Obama, before he leaves office, to send them **$2 billion** more – because after all, remember due to the sanctions imposed by the U.S. and our allies, there are things (like roads, yea roads) they just can't buy. Darn those roads! From looking at Hillary Clinton's history with deal making, I'm pretty sure that if Hillary Clinton becomes President, these types of under-the-table deals will continue. And they will continue to harm America.

I believe that President Obama and Hillary Clinton need to learn the old saying, "Perception is everything." So trying to say, it was all coincidental, when the Iranian press is quoting senior Iranian defense officials who are saying **it was** an exchange for the hostages, assumes that we the American people are what? Stupid? In addition, even if perhaps, in some bizarre way, the universe aligned, and it just happened to coincide on the exact same day, the four hostages were released, then that is very unfortunate. Because due to the law of perception, and due to the Iranian press quoting senior defense officials saying it was ransom; terrorists throughout the world will now assume that we will not only pay ransom, but pay a big ransom at that, flown to then in cash! It's just too darn bad, that like a lot of Americans, the Iranian defense officials, didn't get the memo either, "It's not ransom, stupid. Read my lips!" Do you think it's too late to send the memo out to ISIS, al-Qaeda, and other terrorists around the world?

What I want to know is this, why would President Obama even care about an arms' deal dispute from 1979, with a country that wants nuclear weapons, captures and holds hostages from America and elsewhere, and has vowed to blow Israel off the face of this earth? Why would we want to pay $1.3 billion dollars in interest to a country that supports, trains, hides, and grows terrorists? Why? How can we as a nation, send the best of America off to war to fight terrorism, on the one hand, and then give money – in the form of cash and interest to a country that supports it? I just don't understand this at all.

I realize President Obama, and his team are trying to tell us that it's because our failed arms deal with the Shah of Iraq from 1979 was going before an international tribunal in The Hague. And President Obama and his team were afraid we would lose and have to pay the Iranians even more. I guess this proves what Donald Trump has been saying all along. We are terrible negotiators. If our government believes that an international tribunal is going to say that the United States has to return money that we froze in 1979 to a country that kidnaps and holds our citizens for years, that aggressively supports and supplies terrorists, that wants nuclear weapons, that say 'Death to America,' and that wants to blow Israel off the face of the earth, then we have a serious negotiation problem. And now they have taken three new hostages, since we paid them the ransom, eer…. Excuse me…. gave them cash for their roads. Can we get a refund?

Doesn't it make you wonder, like it did me, how was the United States government able to come up with $400 million dollars in cash, and no agency, no government entity - even reported it missing? If our President can easily hide $400 million dollars, no wonder our country has so much fraud and embezzlement going on.

America's Political System is Broken

Super PACS, a Biased
Media, and Bought
Politicians

America's political system started with anger and a dream. It started with the belief; that people could govern themselves, that we didn't need Kings or Queens, or a ruling party, to rule over us. Our forefathers believed, that they had come up with a system that gave citizens a vote and a voice, in how our country should be governed.

From the beginning, there was discourse, disagreements, and verbal fights, about what our country should look like, how we should govern, who should be or not be, included in our political system, and whose voice mattered. From the beginning, there were nasty fights, outrageous claims, and bold statements made. Nevertheless, through it all, a common ground was reached, agreements were made and a country was formed. No one walked out the door. They stayed and did the important work of forming a new nation. Not because there were no disagreements, not because voices at times were raised, insults thrown, and tempers flared, but because at the end of the day – each side listened, each side gave a little, and the country came out the winner. They realized that our very nation was at stake. They realized that we were a country with divergent views and ideas. They realized that they could not say, 'My way or the highway.' God bless them all.

As explained, in the June 26, 2010 Wall Street Journal, The Saturday Essay titled, *The Feuding Fathers,* by Ron Chernow, George Washington and Thomas Jefferson did not want political parties. George Washington feared that having political parties would lead to party strife, that greatness and rankness and would emerge within the parties as the "worst enemy" to the political system. As Chernow explains, Washington's first cabinet was based on the person's merits not on their political beliefs. However, soon the press joined with the various factions to take sides. Hmmmm.... the press took sides...not much different from today. Two parties with differing views and opinions began to form. And so it was, that political parties were formed with each attacking each other. When attack articles were written, (yes, even back then) no one wrote under their real name, everyone used pseudonyms, that way they didn't have to tell the truth, and they could spin the story any which way they wanted for their own advantage. To think that was over 220 years ago, yet it sounds exactly like today.

Fortunately for America, there were periods of time where a compromise of shorts was reach. Both political parties learned that they needed to work together and reach an agreement that was in the best interest of our country. Over the years, things would get out of whack, and then there would be political strife and dissatisfaction, until it was righted again through the election process. Sometime, look up and read about Theodore Roosevelt and what he had to do to bring our political parties back to our roots.

Our own Constitution was based upon a compromise, called the "Great Compromise" which resolved the issue, among many other things, of congressional representation. Even the six-year term limit for Senators was a compromise. In fact, almost every aspect of our Constitution was reached through, often heated discussions of ideas and opinions, back and forth, until finally a compromise was reached. Without this compromise our Constitution would not have been agreed upon, and we would not exist today.

However, today compromise is seen as a dirty word. Our political congressional districts have been gerrymandered around to the point where ideological opinions are tightly formed and held within each district. Therefore, if a congressman or senator wants to be re-elected, they must hold tightly to the views of the powerful lobbyists, and the ultra-rich who back them financially, or fear losing re-election. Being a right-wing Republican or a left-leaning Democrat currently takes precedent over being an American. In addition, a few very wealthy donors, and strong lobbyist entities, control the process even more tightly than the voting public. They basically say to the candidates, 'If you want my financial assistance in support of your campaign, then this is what I expect out of you. If you do not deliver, then come the next election cycle you're out.' And unfortunately, the ultra-wealthy have the money to throw around, and up until now; they have been able to fool the voting public. Most often, campaigns in the past, have been won by money. The more money put into a campaign, the greater that person's chances of winning. Because the voting public has a bad tendency to believe the negative ads that fill the airways. The more negative ads, the more it appears to the voting public that the ads are true. Political seats in Congress are now considered jobs, actually full-time careers. Everyone wants to be re-elected. They want the paycheck. They want the health benefits. They want the retirement. So they do what is asked of them by their ultra-wealthy donors, while making them constitutes back home believe that they have a voice.

In addition, it seems as if the Democratic party, my former party, wants to divide America. Their message seems to be one where they try to divide the country up by saying, 'If our opponents don't say that something is for one ethnic group or the other, one color of people or the other; then they are against that group of people.' This is not true, and not the way to govern. Groups of people are targeted and courted by give-away programs; no matter the costs. The thing to remember is that not all wealthy individuals try to influence Congress, our President, etc. But those who do, really exert money and power over our elected officials.

There is only one candidate out there who is an outsider, who is not obligated to anyone, and who has proven he has the ability to actually get things done. You don't end up building tremendous hotels, golf courses, and other businesses around the world, unless you have the ability to get things done, to inspire people, and to meet deadlines. Donald Trump has the proven ability to make jobs and build infrastructure. He's done it in private industry, and he can do it for the country. He understands that a strong defense starts with strong borders. I am not saying that Hillary Clinton does not have the ability to get things done. There have been plenty of examples of her getting all kinds of special deals, arrangements, money, etc. for her financial backers and insiders. Don't take my word for it —Google it. Hillary Clinton is the ultimate insider. Hillary knows all games that politicians play. She knows where the money comes from and how to get it. As mentioned, she, President Clinton, and her family's foundation, have taken huge amounts of money, from all kinds of companies, Wall Street investors, foreign governments, and some dictators with horrid civil rights records, and this, in my opinion, makes her ineffective for the change needed in America today, because it would mean starting with herself.

As I was going through this process, and praying about it. I now know that we absolutely need an outsider. We need to send a strong message to Washington that the games have got to stop. Today's politicians, on both sides, are actually trapped. As mentioned above, the way our political system currently works is if they want to keep their job, they can't step outside of their box. It's a travesty really. The political system today is rigged against the average, everyday American. It is rigged financially, and through incentives, to favor those in power and keep them in power. Donald Trump knows this. That is why he was self-funded (along with some donations from everyday Americans) his own campaign during the primary election.

Donald Trump realizes that an outsider, and only an outsider with experience, can turn the country around and get us back to be a nation where everyone wins, not just the wealthy and well-connected. It will take an outsider to get us back to being a nation where there is give and take, and where one side is not constantly winning, and the other side constantly losing. A country where overall, at the end of the day, everyone feels like their voice was heard. A country where we are not afraid to talk about real, honest to goodness, hard issues facing our nation. That we can speak about the issues of illegal immigration, terrorists, immigration, refugees, and money in politics, without being called a racist and worse. And where everyone understands why compromise was used. One where people realize that compromise is not a dirty word, and that talking out loud to each other is not evil, then change is possible. It can happen. It will happen; I believe, if Donald Trump is our next President.

In the past, I've listened to what the candidates have to say and then voted based on who's overall plan for the country, I liked the best. I would watch the debates, listen to the news commentaries, and make up my mind. Sometimes I only paid attention to one main point.

However, now I realize that the political elites were using these one or two-point issues to deflect me from the really underlying and fundamental issues going on in our country. With the main issue being, that we the people are being controlled by a very small group of rich, powerful, special-interest groups and individuals. I came to recognize that, for the most part, the media is feeding us what the politicians want us to hear. Especially in this election, the liberal media, and even the main-stream media, have decided that Donald Trump cannot be President. So, they have set out to sink him, by writing negative article after negative article about him. They take tiny sound bites of what he has said and blow it up, way out of proportion and distort it. The press is being very biased. They want to control this election through the power of persuasion, and they have basically decided Hillary will be our next President; they have crowned her already. And they will ensure it by never giving Donald Trump positive press, and by never giving Hillary Clinton negative press. I hope America catches on to this, and is not swayed but the powers of the media.

For example, Trump said at a rally in Wilmington, N.C., on Tuesday. "By the way, and if she gets to pick her judges, nothing you can do, folks. Although the 2nd amendment people, maybe there is, I don't know." Well, of course the press jumped right on this saying, "Whoa, look at that! Donald Trump is encouraging gun violence against Hillary Clinton! OMG! This is unheard of, jail him! Hang him! String him up by his toes!" And Hillary Clinton in her response tweet, basically accused every person who believes in the 2nd amendment as being willing to commit murder! The media agreed with her. What? That is atrocious! What Hillary Clinton and the media just did was show how biased and bigoted they are against the NRA and people who believe in the right to bear arms. They actually believe that they are so bad, so terrible, so crazy that they would go out and kill a sitting President or Supreme Court nominee! OMG! I can't believe it. I really can't believe it. I support the 2nd amendment, and I don't even own a gun!

I believe that Hillary Clinton, and the media, needs to apologize to every citizen who believes in the 2nd amendment. 2nd amendment people are not murders. They don't own guns, so they can go out and kill people. This is just so ridiculous it needs to just STOP! Calm down. What Donald Trump recognized is that there are strong 2nd amendment people in both parties and in the Independent party. If they joined together and voted for Trump, Hillary wouldn't win the White House. However, even if Hillary does win, Trump still recognizes that the NRA is a strong lobbying unit. They are a cohesive unit, and just like in the past, whenever new gun restriction laws come up, all they have to do is put pressure on the Senate not to vote for a nominee who would not be in favor of the 2nd amendment. I mean, come on people! If something happened to Hillary, her V.P. would take over, and so on. That wouldn't change who was nominated for the Supreme Court. The same party would be in charge; Donald Trump knows this. Give the man some credit. He wasn't advocating gun violence. He was advocating that pressure, by a well-known and organized group, be put on the Senate. The NRA, and its lobbying arm, the Institute for Legislative Action (ILA), is recognized as one of the most powerful special-interest-groups in Washington. They spend $3 million per year on lobbying efforts strictly related to gun policy. They grade Congressmen and women from A to F depending upon their stance on gun laws. On June 20, 2106, their efforts stopped the latest gun reform laws from going into effect, even with the Democratic party's sit-in on the floor of the house. They could, and will easily, be able to pressure Congressmen and women not to vote for a Supreme Court nominee they believe will harm the 2nd amendment.

This was Donald Trump's point, and for commentators and Hillary Clinton to suggest otherwise is reckless. Some commentators went into how such talk can cause an unstable person to try and shoot Hillary Clinton. Donald Trump's words did not say this. The commentators and Hillary Clinton are the ones who put the thought of potential violence into people's heads. Not Donald Trump.

Let's take a look at who is doing the hateful talk. Hillary Clinton and company, including the media, have in my opinion, falsely portrayed Donald Trump as a bigoted racist and more. A man wearing a Trump T-shirt was just beaten with a tire iron. People at Trump rallies are attacked. President Obama said Donald Trump is "unfit for office." The hate speech and negative labels are coming from the Democratic side. This is the speech that will incite violence.

And please, would someone please, explain to me how Hillary Clinton in 2008 could go on TV and say that she is staying in the race just in case Obama gets assassinated like Kennedy did in the month of June! What? Did I just hear that right? Yep, I did. Soooooo, let's get the rules straight; it's ok for the Democratic nominee for President to basically say, 'I'm staying in just in case Barack Obama gets assassinated this month.' But it's not ok, for the Republican nominee to say, "Although the 2nd amendment people, maybe there is, I don't know." Especially when everyone knows full well that the NRA and 2nd amendment people have effectively blocked legislation for years. Unbelievable. The first thing that comes to the media, and Hillary Clinton, is that people who believe in the 2nd amendment are murderers! Really? Seriously? OMG!!! We need an apology! And so does Donald Trump!

For the past several years, even before Donald Trump came along, my husband and I have both watched as our political system has fallen apart. We both recognized that a change was needed. We realized that bi-partisan politics are destroying our country. Big money thrown around by lobbyist, overseas interests, special-interest groups, and Super PACS funded by the ultra-wealthy, have changed our government. Congressmen and women have gerrymandered their districts around to ensure that they, and their party, are voted in repeatedly. We have watched in shock, as good legislation, needed legislation, has been stalled in Washington, due to one-sided politics. We didn't know what to do about it — we felt helpless to change anything. This election has opened our eyes to what is really happening and why.

Have you noticed that what often happens when people are running for office, the first thing they do is take a detailed poll by demographics, and then decided which of the voters they need to target for their votes? Once the poll is done, they develop their targeted 5, 10 or 20 step-plan for fixing everything aimed at that specific group. The targeted polls are used to make up separate plans for each group, and to help them devise a plan aimed strictly at attracting their vote.   For example, take Hillary Clinton's college affordability plan, New College Compact, that is going to cost an estimated $350 billion dollar. Clinton created this plan, so she could compete for young college voters by promising free, or low priced college. It was created to get votes. There is very little chance, in my opinion, of the compact getting passed, because it's a new program that costs billions, and we already have a deficit each year of $534 billion, and almost a $19 trillion-dollar national debt. It was done only to appease the Bernie Sanders' base and generate votes. It's not about doing what is right long term for the American people. It doesn't matter if the new program hampers future generations with large amounts of additional national debt. And it doesn't really matter if it would or would not work. It was all about getting the votes needed to get elected in 2016. Don't forget about the creation of 200,000 jobs in New York that Hillary promised, that never materialized. It my opinion, the Clintons are about the Clintons. Having Hillary win the White House, will greatly improve their financial fortunes. Because boy, are they good at getting people to give them money. Once elected, if President Hillary Clinton, even takes the New College Compact, forward, she'll say, "Well here's my plan, but I couldn't get the Republicans to vote for it, so it's not my fault." Promises are cheap, action is real.

You have probably already heard, about Donald Trump's supposed lack of detail in his plan. You will hear them say that he doesn't offer anything of substance. First off, in a debate you have sometimes 30 seconds to respond, sometimes 90 seconds to 2 minutes to answer a question. Plus, you're being attacked, and you have to address the attack, and then somehow you are supposed to offer detailed steps of your plan that people can understand in the remaining seconds left. You can't really. What Donald Trump is doing, is putting together different teams to address different areas. For example, just recently he revealed in deeper details his economic plan. He has also talked about some of his plans and how he hopes to achieve them in his book *Crippled America*. You can look at them on his website (donaldjtrump.com). He does talk about them during interviews and at rallies, as time and circumstances merit. It seems to me that he has as much out there as Hillary. However, as a way to dismiss him, you will hear the charge that it's not enough. This is an effort to put seeds of doubts in the voters' minds, that he doesn't really have a plan. That he's unqualified. When he is the only one that recognizes, that you need to state the problem, and then work together with both parties and the stakeholders involved, for consensus on a plan created together that will work.

I realize that after reading or perusing this book, you may not agree with me on everything. You may not agree with me on anything! That's ok, that is what America is all about.   We believe in the coming together of ideas, thoughts, dreams, and aspirations. Agreeing at times, and at other times agreeing to disagree. Unfortunately, in our current political system, we have lost the ability to see the other's point of view; we are afraid to speak for fear of being falsely attacked. We no longer argue back and forth, we have lost the ability to reach a compromise where both sides give some, and where at the end of the day we are made stronger for it. When we put America **FIRST**, and political parties second, we as a nation **WIN**. We are after all, all Americans. When we let the press control our thinking through the publishing of biased stories, articles, and newscasts, we all lose.

I believe, it's time to take back our political system and put America first once again. It's time to demand political change. It's time for our elected officials to realize that they work for us, not special-interest groups, or those in the top 1% who are politically involved.

Super PACS

How SuperPACS Have
Changed and Destroyed
Politics Forever

Super PACS were formed after the July 2010 federal court case SpeechNow.org v. Federal Election Commission. Anyone can now form a Super PAC. All that is needed is a letter and the filling out of a couple-page form. After that, Super PACs can accept unlimited contributions from whoever wants to support them, and spend the money however they want, towards any campaign they want, as long as they do not coordinate with the candidate, once the candidate has declared his or her intention to run for office. But, I kinda wonder, who is the watch dog that makes sure they are not coordinating?

As we are now finding out, due to Hillary Clinton's campaign fund (this is not a Super PAC) called *Hillary for America*, there are multiple ways for a campaign to out-maneuver the campaign-finance laws. During the primary Bernie Sanders pointed out that the *Hillary for America* was just a way for Hillary Clinton to skirt campaign-finance laws. Even though, Hillary Clinton **still had five opponents** in the Democratic Primary, by August 2015, at the Democratic National Committee summer meeting, the funding and setting up of the *Hillary for America*, was already being discussed by the leadership of the DNC. By September 10, 2015, it was agreed upon that Hillary's campaign could and would control the finances of the fund.   (This is not common practice). In the past, such agreements are not reached until after the primaries, and after the nomination is secured for a particular candidate. Yet, in my opinion, just like with the Super Delegates, Hillary Clinton, and the

Democratic Party, had already effectively blocked any chance Bernie Sanders, and the other four opponents, had of winning the nomination.

Per the article, "How Do You Build a Political Movement?" in *The Atlantic* by Clare Doran, dated May 3, 2016, Bernie Sanders during his campaign accused Clinton of "looting funds meant for state parties to skirt fundraising limits on her presidential campaign." And it appears; he was totally correct. Per campaign-finance laws, individual donations are limited to $2,700 or $5,400 for married couples. Donations to the National Committees, of either party, are limited to $33,400, and each state involved can get $10,000. There were 32 states that agreed to join the *Hillary for America* campaign. If a person donated to each state, that alone would total $320,000/year. As stated in the article, what Hillary Clinton did through her *Hillary for America*, was to enable rich donors to skirt campaign finance law, and donate upwards of $700,000 to her campaign, by donating $350,000 in 2015 ($2,700 to Hillary, $33,400 to DNC, $320,000 to the states = $356,100) and then donate again, in 2016.

In an attempt to satisfy the law, at some point the money was electronically deposited in each of the 32 state's campaign accounts, but then just as quickly the funds were electronically sent back to the DNC. Sometimes it happened so quickly that the states involved didn't even know they had received any money. When questioned, the DNC said, 'Oh they could have kept whatever they needed, but they didn't need it so they sent it back.' Ok... However, other people involved stated they knew all along they weren't able to keep it. In the end, the money designated to go to the 32 states and the DNC, instead went to Hillary's campaign. You can read about it in the May 2, 2016 article, "Clinton fundraising leaves little for state parties" as reported in *Politico,* written by Kenneth Vogel and Isaac Arnsdort. Their research found that 99% of the money was going to Clinton, and only 1% was going to the states! So, by skirting the intention of the law, Hillary Clinton was able to turn a limit of $5,400 into $700,000! Hillary, and her very rich friends and supporters, used this method to raise millions of millions of dollars. And this doesn't even begin to count the separate money that is going to Super PACS.

Since their creation, Super PACS have quickly risen to have unprecedented influence in our political process and elections. There are approximately 2,200 Super PACS in existence.   As of July 23, 2016, according to OpenSecrets.org, so far Super PACS have raised $936,510,815. Almost a billion dollars! Of the 2,200 Super PACS, the majority of money was raised and spent by 50 Super PACS. For example, the *Right to Rise USA* Super PAC, which supported Jeb Bush before he dropped out of the race, raised $121,145,774. *Priorities USA Action* Super PAC so far has raised $100,040,922 for Hillary Clinton.   One hundred million dollars! Hillary Clinton has three main Super PACS supporting her. They are: *Priorities USA*, listed above at $100,040,922, *Correct the Record* raised to date:

$6,384,152. *Ready PAC* raised to date: $3,528,959. And her campaign fund (not officially a Super PAC) *Hillary for America* raised to date $264,374,319.

Altogether, twenty-five individuals and companies have donated anywhere from $10,000,000 to $1,000,000, and 45 individuals and companies, have donated from $500,000 to $250,000 to Super PACS. Talk about the top 1%. Do you really believe that they want nothing in return? A review of the records indicates they are mainly made up of hedge funds, Wall Street investment companies, health companies, energy companies, and other large corporations.

Haim Saban, who has businesses related to financial services, entertainment, and media, has donated just over $10 million dollars to date to Hillary Clinton. He's worth $3.4 billion, so this is like peanuts for him. Or more explicitly, it would be similar to a person earning $60,000/year donating $200. He has donated to the Clintons for years. When Bill Clinton was President, he rewarded him by having him sit on his Export Council.

Renaissance Technologies is an investment management firm. James Simons, Founder and Board Chair, donated just over $9.5 million to a Super PAC supporting Hillary. He was charged with cheating on taxes through his hedge fund by writing a program that made it appear that ordinary income, which should have been taxed at the full rate, was instead magically transferred and categorized as capital gains and only taxes at 15%. This cost the American government $6 billion dollars in taxes! Even so, the Clinton's still hang with him and freely accept his money. Currently, Renaissance Technologies have assets of $65 billion under their management.

Paloma Partners, also a financial management company, headed by Donald Sussman, has to date donated just over $6.1 million to one of Hillary's Super PACS. One of his companies was accused of a bribery scandal in the Virgin Islands. Paloma Partners, worth over $2 billion, received $200 million of US taxpayer funds as part of the AIG bailout. Are you starting to see the pattern? It appears to me, that the Clintons have no problem, let me repeat that, no problem, taking money from people who find ways to skirt or bend or possibly bribe their way to richness. And the rest of us wonder, why the 1% keep getting richer, and we stagnate.

To date, eighteen other individuals or companies have given between $7.5 million and $1.5 million to Hillary Clinton. Secrets.org has an excellent website where you can look candidates and Super PACS up to get this information.

What a lot of people may not realize is that Super PACS are basically accountable to NO ONE. Well, ok, they have to file receipts (money brought in) and disbursements (money spend) reports with the Federal Elections Commission. Secret.org puts each Super PAC's reports on the Internet. That's basically the end of the accountability. A person or persons could complain to the FEC, but like that would go anywhere. The Clinton's are never charged or indicted for anything. They have an *in* with Loretta Lynch, U.S. Attorney General, remember? She won't even look into the Clinton Foundation, and we all remember the email server non-indictment after meeting with Bill on her plane...

Super PACS can accept unlimited amounts of money from anyone who wants to donate to their cause. They can create and pay for ads and airtime. The only thing they are not allowed to do is cover basic campaign expenses such as salaries for staff, travel costs, event fees, and anything else that is done by the candidate's campaign committee.

As mentioned earlier, the candidate's official campaign committee is limited to a maximum donation of $2,700 per person for the primary elections, and another $2,700 for the general election. This is what got Jeb Bush into trouble. He had huge Super PACS supporting him, but he did not have the everyday person sending in money to support his official campaign. Too bad he didn't follow the *Hillary for America* method of skirting campaign finance laws, and transfer monies donated to RNC and the states to his own campaign. Instead, he ran out of money to pay for staff, offices, etc.

Unfortunately, the lesson campaigns are learning from Super PACS is that the best way to get donations is to be as negative and polarizing as possible. It is well known, that when you send out flyers, letters, emails or phone calls, attacking your opponent, you can receive three times as much money as you receive when you send out the same flyer, letter, or email, praising yourself or your party. Polarization pays; nothing unites like a common enemy.

Since 2010, independent spending by Super PACS has skyrocketed. It appears, there is no stopping them. Political consultants love it. And now one of the most fundamental parts of our election process, the funding of campaigns, and the message that is sent to the voters, has been hijacked by the ultra-rich. I believe, that in the process, democracy has been lost, our elected officials no longer represent "we the people," they represent the wealthy donors who will kick in the money to fund their campaigns. Mike Huckabee's comment to Fox News was to follow the money. Sounds like Watergate doesn't it?

This is truly the top 1% ruling America. And this is one of the primary reasons that Donald Trump self-funded his primary campaign. He knows that in order to be effective he has to be free of obligations and favors so that he can do what is right for the people of America, not the wealthy few, or the special interests, or the most vocal, etc.

By being free of special interest, wealthy backers, and corporate entities, Donald Trump will be able to make deals and reach workable compromises that will be in the best interest of all Americans. He realizes that compromise is not a bad thing. You just have to know where the line is that you are unwilling to cross and have an end-game and outcome in mind. Donald Trump has stated many times that making a deal is hard work. It takes effort, patience and understanding. It's far easier to walk away and fold your arms and not even try. However, then nothing gets done. America and Americans are hurt, and our country loses. By being willing to find common ground, things get done, jobs get created, infrastructures get repaired, vets get the help they need, tax law gets simplified and overhauled. In addition, the military gets the funding, and backing needed to destroy radical Islamic extremists; our national debt gets reduced; campaign finance reform is achieved; and so on. Donald Trump has made deals his whole life. It's time now for him to make them for the benefit of the American people. The main reason he will be able to effectively do this is because he is not indebted to anyone. He is willing to bluntly speak his mind. He can and will put the interests of the American people first. Not special interests, not lobbyist, not Super PACS, not wealthy individuals, or companies clamoring for special deals. He will be the first President, probably since George Washington, to actually work for the American people.

A New York Times article by Nicholas Confessore, Sarah Cohen, and Karen Yourish dated August 1, 2015, titled 'Small Pool of Rich Donors Dominates Election Giving,' found that fewer than 158 families raised almost half of the money for the 2016 presidential campaigns to date. The same three authors, also wrote another New York Times article, dated Oct. 10, 2015, called 'Buying Power'. Both are worth reading. I'm sure that since these articles were written, the amount of money donated has only increased. Thank you Super PACS! That is a scary, scary thing. There are 319 million people living in the United States. In 2012, there were 235 million people of voting age in the U.S. In 2016, 158 ultra-wealthy families, along with 536 politicians (535 voting members of Congress and one President), for a total of 694 people, are trying to control the destiny of 319 million people. If we sit back, they win. If we rise up and vote for Donald Trump, we can send a powerful message to Washington, that we want our country back.

During Hillary Clinton's primary-night acceptance speech, she said the following, "I applaud Sen. Sanders and his millions of supporters for wanting to get unaccountable money out of our politics and giving greater emphasis to closing the gap of inequality." Yet, while she mouths these words, she is using her own *Hillary for America* to skirt them, and she continues to accept donations from the same wealthy donors and Wall Street investment firms that have always supported her. She is talking out of both sides of her mouth. It appears that she will applaud them, while choosing to bend the laws herself. Do as I say, not as I do!

As you go into this election, remember this: Donald Trump has not taken money from special interests. He did not have the backing of super delegates sewn up before the primaries. He has not exploited the Campaign-Finance laws for his own personal campaign. He has not taken millions of dollars from foreign corporations, governments and dictatorships. He does not support the Panama Free Trade Agreement, as currently written. So, what every Bernie Sanders supporter has to ask themselves is this – do these things matter or not? Do you want a person in the White House, who will keep an Oligarchy/Plutocracy form of government in existence, or do you want to give control of the government of the United States back to the people where it rightly belongs? If you believe that the government is supposed to be for the people, of the people, and by the people, then you need to vote for Donald Trump.

It's Getting Ugly and It's Gonna Get Uglier!

Here Comes the Mud, Slings, and Arrows

Now that the some of the old-guard Republican and Democratic plutocrats, know that Donald Trump will not go silently in the night, they are getting scared. They don't want to lose their power, and they want to keep things going the way they want. They want to stack the system in their favor. They want to keep telling the American people their narrative of how things are. The point is, that a lot of Americans, just like me, want a new narrative, a new direction, and new leadership.

Between now and the election, it's going to get even muddier, meaner, and nastier. The press will be right in the thick of it. They will do all they can to sink Donald Trump. So, expect it all to be blamed on Trump. Expect to hear over and over again how unfit, unprepared, and how terrible Donald Trump will be as President. Does this scare you, and make you think they are right? It shouldn't. Please keep reading.

Have you seen the meme on the Internet where they show Donald Trump as basically a big mouth with hair? That's ok, but pointing out the real problems in America is not? Or how about the movie that was made using *Game of Thrones* where they take Donald Trump words and put him into the video with totally different circumstances and make him appear to be a bad ruler? The video would have you believe that if we build a wall, and actually made people enter our country legally; they would all starve to death and die. Really? People from Mexico and South America will starve to death? They are not coming here because they are going to starve to death, they are coming here because they want to earn more money. Have you also seen or heard about the mental-health "experts," who without even examining Donald Trump diagnosed him as narcissistic? This is so so wrong and totally unprofessional. They got their info about him from watching 20-second sound bites on TV. Yea, that's professional. Dr. Robert Klitzman, from Columbia University, pointed out that such behavior is unethical, per the rules of the American Psychiatric Association.

As it has just recently been divulged by WikiLeaks and the DNC email scandal, it appears that members of the DNC lead by Debbie Wasserman Schultz purposely and intentionally tried to circumvent the will of the people in this election process and destroy democracy by sabotaging Bernie Sanders' campaign. They purposely put out false and misleading information about Bernie Sanders to benefit Hillary Clinton. Debbie Wasserman Schultz, under pressure from Bernie Sanders, resigned as Chairman of the DNC and was promptly hired by Hillary Clinton and her campaign for a job well done! I don't know if I'm alone in this, but this seems incredibly wrong to me. Instead of Hillary Clinton speaking out against the undermining of Bernie Sanders' campaign and the undermining of democracy, she instead openly rewarded the head person responsible for trying to circumvent democracy in America. She rewarded the one person, in charge of those trying to undo the will of the voters, in this election process. I ask you, does the end always justifies the means? If so, why are we anywhere in the world right now fighting for freedom? If we cannot uphold the values of freedom, truth, righteousness, and 'we the people' here at home, how can we even dare pretend we are fighting for it elsewhere? It seems to me that we are undermining our own political process, and we need to withdraw all of our troops from around the world, and quit playing the game of the greatest protectors of freedom and equality – ever. Because if it doesn't apply here, in our own country, with the Democratic Party, then how can we make it apply anywhere? I can only assume that the Democratic party was too afraid to let the voting process occur unfiltered. Too afraid that Hillary Clinton might lose, unless they circumvented Bernie Sanders' campaign. Just like the liberal and mainstream media is too afraid to let the voting process proceed normally, instead they have chosen themselves to be the designated destroyers of all things Trump.

It is now crystal clear to me, why God wanted me to vote for Donald Trump. The Democratic party just proved to the world, that they do not believe in or support democracy. They do not believe in or support the will of the people. They do not believe in or support a free voting process. They do not believe in or support majority rule by the people, for the people, of the people. They believe in the exact opposite of what they have been telling people all along. And so do the liberal and majority of the mainstream press. They believe in a plutocracy, oligarchy form of government, where the rich and the political elite control the government, and the government exist primarily for their benefit.

To make matters even worse, in my opinion, the Democratic Party is now trying to spin the email leak and blame it all on Donald Trump and the Russians. They are not addressing the actual subject matter and intention that the leak revealed, instead they are trying to spin it to say, "how terrible the Russians are in cahoots with Donald Trump, and they did this to try and sabotage Hillary's chances of being President. How dare they!" Donald Trump and the Russians, yea right. I ask you, who wrote the contents of the emails? Who questioned Bernie Sanders' religion and questioned his faith? Who made fun of a black supporter's name? Who developed a system within the Democratic Party for rewarding rich donors with back scratching and favoritism? Donald Trump and the Russians did not develop the Democratic Party's system of supporting Wall Street and the ultra-rich in America. They did not run the polls and focus groups to develop the rhetoric whereby they could say anything they wanted, by specific group, down to even saying what horse-lovers want to hear, all to the justification of the end – getting elected. Where, once elected, it will be back to conducting business as usual.

But, now I think the scariest thing of all has just happened. One of the young DNC staffers, who had worked for the DNC for two years as a Voter Expansion Data Director, was gunned down in Washington, D.C. as he was returning to his house around 4 am. The police said it was robbery gone bad, but his father disagrees because nothing was stolen from him, not his wallet, not his cell phone, not his watch. It is also interesting to note that WikiLeaks founder, Julian Assange, just offered a $20,000 reward to anyone with information on his murder. Remember WikiLeaks posted the DNC emails. I don't know, but to me, it's scary to think that someone was murdered for revealing what was actually going on in the DNC. The police, however, feel certain that it was a robbery gone awry, because the area where he lived was having a spat of robberies lately. Let's us hope that is what it was, because the other suggestion is just too unfathomable.

I do have to admit that I laughed when Donald Trump came out, looked straight-faced into the camera, and asked the Russians to hack Hillary Clinton's server and turn over her 30,000 missing emails. The Democrats and the press were absolutely horrified by this comment, how dare a candidate for President of the United States, encourage another country to hack us! President Obama came out and said he was "unfit for the office." Well, come on, I believe that anyone who gets Donald Trump, gets that this was done very tongue-in-cheek, as a response to their totally bogus and false charges that he is in cahoots with the

Russians to sabotage Hillary's changes of winning this election. It's so ridiculous; it's funny. We all know the hard drive was destroyed. The server has been taken down, and the emails were shredded. Right, Hillary? That's what you told us. Donald Trump knows this too; it was done to point out the absurdity of their claim pointing to him for the DNC email-hack. They are trying to deflect the contents of the emails, into how horrible that we were hacked and Donald Trump, and the Russians did it! And the press is playing right along with them!

Donald Trump is running as the only true Washington outsider; he is the only one willing not to sell out. His goals are different from every politician. He is the only one to continue to voice the corruption in our political system due to years of the ultra-wealthy and political elite controlling our election and political processes. You may have noticed that during the election, he was the one standing up for Bernie Sanders, and voicing his concerns from the beginning, that the DNC was trying to rig the system and take away the voice of the people. He is the one who pointed out how wrong it was for Hillary Clinton to have all the bound delegates, before the primaries even started. He pointed out how the Republican process was biased against outsiders; like himself. He pointed out how big-money donors were backing political establishment figures like Jeb Bush. Again and again, he was the voice calling for reform in Washington.

Yet, unbelievable to my ears, Bernie Sanders stood on the stage of the Democratic National Convention and stated that Hillary Clinton, the one ultimate political insider of all insiders, was the only person in America, who could fix our problems.   Why did he do this? I don't know for sure, but it appears to me that in his mind, the end justifies the means. He got some concessions in the platform (which goes nowhere and was specially meant to attract his supporters.) And for those concessions, he was willing to overlook, and throw away American democracy. Something that 1,354,664 Americans have died defending, and 1,498,237 Americans have been injured defending, since our country was formed. I believe that his sellout can never ever be justified.

So, I ask you this? Where is the outrage by the press? Except for Fox News, Breitbart.com, and a few other online conservative news agencies, nowhere to be seen. Why? Because as shown by the DNC email hack, the press is by-and-large behind Hillary for President. It appears, that the DNC fed CNN news the questions to ask Hillary during their interviews. It appears they told reporters when to tone down their comments, and what to leave out. The DNC worked with the political commentators from the majority of news networks (except Fox). They edited news reporters' articles before they were submitted, and it goes on. I use to like to watch CNN. I use to like to watch ABC news. I will never watch those stations again. This to me is horrifying that the press in America would try to purposely make one candidate appear more favorably than the other on their newscasts. We are not taking about during paid TV shows, but on their newscasts. No wonder so many people no longer trust the news in America. I do have to admit that in the past, I could blatantly see that some people were pro one side or the other, but I never assumed that the moderators and main political news reporters were this way too. I hate to admit how ignorant I was. A good summary source on the WikiLeaks/DNC emails can be found here: http://www.thegatewaypundit.com/2016/07/detailed-list-findings-wikileaks-dnc-document-dump/.

During the early part of the primaries, Hillary Clinton and the Democratic party railed against the G.O.P. for having a field of Presidential candidates who were pushing for tax plans that favored the rich, and wanted to decimate regulations for wealthy companies. They complained that some of the RNC candidates were receiving millions upon millions of dollars in Super PAC contributions from the Koch brother and others, and who were trying to "buy up the political system." Well, guess what? They are ALL gone! The only Republican candidate still standing did **none** of those things. This is so important for this election. Donald Trump did none of these things. There is only one candidate left in this race, who has done exactly what the DNC and Hillary Clinton railed against in the primaries and that person is, Hillary Rodham Clinton. Hillary Clinton, through her Super PACS and *Hillary for America* campaign fund has brought in so far $374,328,353! More than any other candidate in the history of our electoral process. *The Bill, Hillary, and Chelsea Clinton Foundation* have taken in over $2 billion dollars to date, not all of it from the nicest people in the world. A major portion of the donations to their foundation has been made by foreign donors, some of whom were countries and dictators around the world whose treatments of women, girls, minorities, and LGBT individuals are beyond atrocious.

A few, important sounding individuals, like a Harvard Professor (impressive, right?), Rachel Maddow (a left wing news-show host), and Sam Altman (an ultra-wealthy venture capitalist), all of whom support Hillary Clinton; have stated that Donald Trump is the next Hitler. It appears, to me, that they are trying to instill fear in voters by comparing Trump's rise to that of Hitler's. This is fear mongering at it's worse. Please, say what? Trump is not saying, let's annihilate a group of innocent people. He is saying radical Islamic jihadist extremists have vowed to destroy us. They have vowed to destroy Christianity. They have vowed to do, whatever is necessary, and whatever they can, to kill every last one of us, and everyone around the world, who does not bow down to their extreme view of religion. In the world of radical jihadist extremists, its ok to rape women, slash the heads off of Christians, kidnap innocent people for ransom, kidnap innocent girls to sell or force into marriage or sex, and kill girls and women who want to go to school. In their world, Harvard would not be able to accept female students; schools for girls would not exist. Education for women would not exist. This is not made-up. This is real.

Donald Trump is NOT Hitler. His rise is because people in the United States of America have had enough, and know that he is the person who can, and will do, whatever is necessary to enable our military to defeat ISIS and other terrorist organizations, by giving them the resources needed to protect America from radical jihadist extremists; build back our economy; create jobs; and give **EVERYONE** a chance, once again, at the American Dream.

I would compare the popularity of Donald Trump more to Winston Churchill. Winston Churchill took the lead in warning about Nazi Germany. He also warned about the 'Iron Curtain' of the Soviet Union long before it was popular to do so. He was, like Trump, blunt and said what he meant. He inspired the British people to have hope and to keep on fighting during WWII. Trump is giving people hope today, telling us that we can and will defeat radical jihadist extremists; that we will be a country that, once again, creates well-paying jobs; that we will have a health care system which works for all; that our soldiers, once they have fought for us and return home, broken of body and limb, will be honored and cared for. That as a country, we will not abandon them. Our veterans, who gave so much to our country, will receive the care, they need to heal their minds and bodies, learn how to function without their limbs, and be able to hold their heads up high, and know that we value them. They were there for us, and we will be there for them. He is the only candidate talking about the need for intensive drug rehabilitation programs, not prisons for people caught up in the drug epidemic.

The main thing for Trump supporters, those who are thinking of maybe voting for Trump, and those who are still undecided on how to vote, is to remember this: why are so many of the political elite and Super PACS afraid of Donald Trump? Is it because they really care about the welfare of you and me? It is because they really think, he will be worse than any President we have ever had? Or is it really because they want to keep the power, the control, and the rewards that they have come to love and depend upon so much? I believe it is the latter.

For many politicians, being a politician is their job. They like being an elected official with power. They like the money and the benefits. They like the power. They want to stay in for as long as possible, because it pays well and what else would they do? Some ex-politicians will go on to become lobbyists; some will go to think tanks; some will go to law firms, where they will use their inner circle within the political process to get concessions and deals for their clients. However, for most, this job is probably the best job they will ever have, and they want to keep it.

Sometimes, I wonder if I am listening to the same broadcast, the same speech or debate, as the "political analysts," or if they just do it on purpose. I have heard analyst after analyst say that Donald Trump if elected will rule with an iron fist, he will be worse than Obama at using executive orders. He will just decree it so. I stare at them and wonder, where on God's green earth did that get that from? And now I realize it is because they are so anti-Trump that they have truly lost their objectivity. They aren't analysts; they are truth spinners.

If you have studied Donald Trump, listened to what he says, read his book *Crippled America*, and read about him, you would know this is hogwash. It is so far from the truth that it makes me want to pull my hair out! Donald Trump has said over and over again, that it's all about negotiation and deal making. It's all about meeting with Congress. It's all about getting together with his advisors. It's all about finding the absolutely best solution that will work. He has stated that he has his starting point, and he knows the end objective that he wants to reach, but then he knows it will take sitting down with members of Congress and hashing out the fine details. But as we now know the Democrats, some political analysts, and anti-Trump Super PACS, along with a large part of the media (who have already decided to crucify Trump) will twist the truth and tell you otherwise. Not because it is the truth, but because they want to keep Congress, our government, our economic system, and their political ties for themselves.

Whereas, these same people, don't seem bothered when Hillary Clinton comes right out, as she did with her immigration reform package, and say she will use executive order to implement as many parts of it as she can to make it happen.

Trump is in some pretty good company when it comes to being blasted by the press, the political parties, and political pundits for being horrible. Here are some examples:

When President Lincoln ran for office in 1860, he was described as a 'fool, an idiot, an ape" (Swint, 2006:194). In 1864 when running for reelection it got worse, then he was called a 'filthy storyteller, a liar, a thief, a braggart, a buffoon, a perjurer, a swindler, a tyrant, and a butcher' (Boller, 2004: 115). It would appear to me that Donald Trump is in some pretty good company.

Romney did not attend the Republican National Convention and beforehand was attacking Trump as a fraud and a con man. You've probably heard about it. Super PACS supporting Hillary have come out with vicious ads repeating the same spin. Hillary Clinton recently came out and stated that during his 30-year career Donald Trump, has been involved in 3,500 lawsuits. She made it appear that the majority of these were due to him fighting everyday people in an effort to take away or keep what he owed them. It would appear that she purposely maligned the facts and distorted the truth to make it appear that Donald Trump was not a champion of the people.

I have a question, have you ever heard of a real fraudster fighting back? Typically, if a person was a fraud, they don't want to fight the case in court forever, as has been the case with Trump. They make a deal and go quietly into the night, looking for their next victim. They certainly don't spend millions fighting the case. Or allow the case to go on during their run for President of the United States. Instead, they reach a settlement, and have all parties sign a non-disclosure agreement.

I'm sure that with Trump University, there were people out there who were unhappy with the course. They were hoping to make millions, like Trump. Some of the courses were offered during the real estate downturn, and unless you have nerves of steel like Trump, you're probably not going to take a huge leap of faith, buy properties, or make lots of money during that time. I doubt that Trump's meaning was to defraud them, but what the salespeople/instructors of the class said, who knows? Some of the unhappy participants, now suing, said they wrote a good review at the end of the course, because the instructors said if they didn't they wouldn't get rehired. What? If they weren't happy, if they felt they did not get their money's worth, it seems to me that they just did a huge disservice to Trump. How was he to know, if they liked the class or not, if the instructors were good or not, if they give a good review? They waited, and now months or years later, they say it was terrible. Some, it appears, didn't even decide this until they were contacted about joining in a class-action lawsuit.

So I guess my point with all of this is, don't assume and don't believe what a person's political opponent wants you to believe. They want us to believe Trump is a racist, a demigod, a fraudster, a con artist, or any of a number of other negative labels they have thrown at him (just like the labels thrown at President Lincoln 150 years ago) in a desperate attempt to stay in power. Just, remember there can be lots of reasons, why some of the people who took the courses, later decided they were unhappy. But, to claim that Trump was ripping off the poor, the elderly, is wrong. Anyone who goes into a presentation like this needs to analyze what is being said, with their heads on straight, can I afford to pay this money or not? Think time-share presentations and real estate classes all across the country. No one can twist another person's arm. The person made the decision on their own, for their own reasons, and if the salesmen used pressure tactics or lied to them, then that needs to be put squarely on the shoulders of the salesperson and instructors, and on the people themselves, who caved to their pressure tactics, it would seem to me. I have actually read reviews from people who have praised the courses they took through Trump University. They stated they felt the money was well worth the investment, and changed their lives. So, I agree with Trump's latest statement, he disagrees with the lawsuits, he is fighting them, and the courts will have to decide.

In addition, Mitt Romney (whose words, I'm sure, will now be used by Hillary and the Democratic political machine) has carried it one step further by coming out and saying that Donald Trump besides being a fraud and a con man, is a failure, due to Trump Airlines, Trump Vodka, Trump Steaks, and Trump Mortgage. I guess that Romney forgot the fact that the shame is not in trying and losing, the shame is in never trying at all. Trump has tried lots of things. Not all worked out. Well good for him, at least he was trying to expand the economy. At least, he was trying to create jobs. Most of Trump's efforts succeeded; a few didn't. That's the way of business. At least, Donald Trump didn't cannibalize companies like Mitt Romney did to make his money. You want to know why Mitt Romney lost his Presidential bid, because Romney made millions by raiding American companies. His company, Bain Capital, made Romney a rich man by borrowing vast sums of money in the companies' name, then taking a large cut, and leaving if for other people to pay back, or for the company to file bankruptcy. Check out Matt Taibbi's article in Rolling Stone called "Greed and Debt: The True Story of Mitt Romney and Bain Capital."

I am sure you have probably also heard the accusation from a number of people, that Trump didn't create his wealth; he inherited it. It was reported that when

Fred Trump, died in 1999, he was worth $200-$300 million. Trump has said that years earlier his dad gave him one million to start his first real estate venture, and from there he continued to grow and expand. When Donald Trump's father died, not all of his father's money, would have been given to Donald. His mother was still alive. In addition, Donald had three other living siblings at that time. They would have gotten their share also. Even if he inherited $75 million, he still turned that into $9 billion. So…. you decide. They also like to say that if he had invested it in Wall Street, $300 million would be $9 billion today, or some stupid argument like that, so see he inherited it. OMG. Guess what, he didn't invest it in Wall Street, he took it and built things! He built hotels and golf courses, etc. that actually employ people, a lot of people. Amazing how people will twist and turn things to attack a political opponent.

Have you also, seen the ads saying he's racist? The ads say his dad was a member of the KKK (there is no proof of this whatsoever). Here's my take on that. Trump is not a racist; he is just like I am, and countless other Americans. People who have known him for years, vouch for him and say that he is anything but a racist. He is against drug dealers, criminals, terrorist, and people who want to harm America. If you listen to his speeches, he has said over and over again, that he is all for and supports legal immigrants. He likes people of all ethnic groups. He likes people from Mexico. He likes Muslims. He has friends and employees who are from Mexico, and many friends who are Muslims.

He does not agree with **illegal immigration**, because it leaves the country open to drug dealers who are destroying town after town, criminals of all types, jihadists, organized crime, and others to easily come into our country. Suddenly now, everyone who doesn't support illegal immigration is a racist? That is just amazing to me, because I don't support illegal immigration, and I'm not a racist. I have more Hispanic friends, than white friends. Some of my closet friends and co-workers were black. I had a choice of two high-schools to send my children to. One was primarily white. The other was a highly diverse school. We chose the diverse high school because we wanted our children to meet people and become friends with people from all races, and they have.

To say a person in racist because they are against **ILLEGAL** immigration is just crazy. Really, am I a racist because I'm against drugs? Am I a racist because I'm against the exploitation of illegal immigration? Am I a racist because I'm against children being taken advantage by greedy, mean, unscrupulous people once they get here? Am I racist because I want there to be a system where people can legally come to our country and are held accountable once here? Am I racist because I want to know how many people are actually in our country and from where? Am I racist because I don't want to see young girls sold into slavery once they are here, or forced to work in sweatshops for low or no wages, because they can't speak up for fear of being deported? Am I racist because I want the people who were born here, or who entered our country legally, not to have to compete for jobs with those who enter illegally and will work for less?

Unless you answered yes to the above, then just remember that just because a person calls someone something and puts a label on them, doesn't make it true. Just because others want to name call, Donald Trump, and try to label him a racist, a bigot, and so on doesn't make it true. Just because Donald Trump pointed out the truth that **some** people in the Muslim religion are jihadists and Islamic terrorists, and **some** people coming into the country illegally are rapist and drug dealers, doesn't mean he is saying that **all** are.

Presidents Lincoln and Jefferson both filed for personal bankruptcy, Jefferson several times. President William McKinley filed for bankruptcy twice. Donald Trump has never personally filed for bankruptcy. Businesses, operated under the Trump name, filed for bankruptcy in order to refinance debt and stay alive during the downturn in Atlantic City. In some ways, I believe that having this experience will better equip a President Trump to deal with our own National Debt of $19 trillion dollars and growing daily. He knows, from a business perspective that too much debt is not a good thing.

I'm sure you have seen the ads attacking Donald Trump because he has his suits and ties made in China and

Mexico. The ads state that if Trump was for the American workers, he would make his ties and suits here. To me, that shows they don't understand the problem, and that is what this election is all about. It's clear they really don't understand how business works. That is the exact problem that Trump has been talking about. The problem is that the Chinese, for example, manipulate their currency levels and do other things to the point where it is not economical for American businesses to compete with them. That is why Trump wants to change our agreements with them. The problem is not that Donald Trump doesn't make his suits and ties in the United States; the overarching problem is why he can't make them in the United States profitably. The Chinese government purposely manipulates the variables so that the United States cannot compete – irrespective of labor costs. We need a President who understands all the factors involved. Not someone who will just reiterate the positions of the political establishment, and hopes that the American people, will be content enough to just shut up, and let them do what they want to stay in power and run America the way they want.

During the primaries, it came out that back in the 1979-1980 a contractor hired by Donald Trump, to demolish a building, hired both union workers and 200 non-union workers. The non-union workers were known as the Polish Brigade because they came from Poland. The union filed a lawsuit, against a union boss, the contractor, and Donald Trump. As we all know, lawyers follow the money and always sue the person with the most money. The union boss, even if found guilty wouldn't have a huge amount of money. The contractor probably wasn't as rich as Donald Trump, so Donald Trump was included in the lawsuit. Just to be clear, the suit wasn't brought by the polish workers, who worked off the CONTRACTOR'S books seven days a week, 12 hours a day for $4-$5/hour. As a reference, the average wages for all U.S. workers, at that time, was about $6.50/hour. Trump argued that he was not the one that hired the workers, the contractor did. And actually that is how a construction contract works. Unless you are an owner-builder which I believe, Donald Trump was not, you hire a contractor to do whatever is covered by the contract for an arranged price within a set timeline. The contractor then hires the people to make it happen. The contractor receives payments by the owner for meeting certain deadlines, and the contractor pays the workers. In this case, because the contract deadline was so tight, the contractor hired both union and non-union employees. The contractor decided to bring in 200 workers from Poland to work on the job. The union wanted $1 million dollars. In 1994, a judge ruled that Trump should have known, even though he was not the person who hired them. He was ordered to pay $325,000 plus interest and attorney's fees and costs. Trump appealed on principle. Stating again, he did not know. He did not hire the workers. He decided to fight it because he strongly believed that he was not the employer, he did not do the hiring. No one had told him or sought his approval, to hire illegal workers. The case went on for another five years, until it was settled in 1999. The terms of the settlement are sealed; therefore, no one knows how much he had to pay, if anything. It was a civil lawsuit where damages would be claimed by one side, and the other side would be required to pay, if found responsible. In addition, there were three defendants so each would have been liable for whatever portion was deemed responsible to them. It would appear, just based upon the cost of fighting legal cases, that Donald Trump believed enough about his position that he spent way more over the years in lawyer fees, fighting this case than it would have cost him to settle it.

It is interesting to note that since that time, Donald Trump has been accused by the press, the ultra-wealthy, and Democratic guard, of hiring illegal workers on his current sites; but none have ever been found. He has denied this. On the campaign trail when a reporter said he heard that he has illegal immigrants working on one of his sites. Donald Trump questioned the reporter and asked, "Who?" Then he went on to tell him to give him the name or names, and he will see that they are fired immediately. He further stated that he did not know of any illegal immigrants working at any of his sites or in any of his companies. He stated that he uses an independent contracting firm to verify that all the workers, working on any of his sites, have the legal status and documentation to legally work in the U.S. And again, he reiterated to everyone there, that if they found someone to let him know, and they will be let go immediately. One person, did get interviewed by a reporter and said that he was working at one of Donald Trump's sites, and he was here illegally. He was smirking about it. So, if true, how did this happen? The only way he could have been verified to legally work in the United States, is through the use of identity theft (stealing a U.S. citizen's Social Security number) and the use of a phony green card.   Unfortunately, the private contracting firm hired by Donald Trump to screen employees probably was not able to tell that the person was using a stolen social security number and a fake green card. The individual involved, seemed to be proud of the fact that he was using a stolen social security number and fake green card. Wow, just wow. The problem on the part of the employment verification companies is that the Social Security Administration cannot notify companies about stolen numbers. They can't even notify the real person whose number was stolen!

I actually think that this lawsuit, and the issues it brings up, make Donald Trump a stronger candidate for President. I think this is why he wants to solve the illegal immigration problem.   He knows, first hand, that contractors and companies will hire the workers willing to work for the lowest wages. Which ends up taking away work from legal citizens living here in the United States.

It is his dogged determination to fight for what he believes in that makes him the best Presidential candidate out there, we need someone willing to go to bat for us and not willing to give up. Don't let the Anti-Trump Super PACS, Hillary Clinton, the Never Trumpers, or the unbelievably biased media, paint Donald Trump with a broad brush of accusations that just don't apply. Or, as in this case, accuse him and leave out all the details, just saying enough to smear without the facts or truth being told.

On August 3, 2015, Jim Meyers posted an article on http://www.newsmax.com entitled '15 Things Trump and Reagan Have in Common.' I encourage you to look it up and read it. In summary, he said:

> ➢ Reagan and Trump are both considered Washington outsiders.
> ➢ Reagan was dismissed as a serious candidate. Reagan was ridiculed, and everyone said he could not win. Sound familiar?
> ➢ The establishment and many others attacked Reagan and now are attacking Trump for being extreme and without a 'real' plan or policy.
> ➢ Reagan was criticized and blasted when he signed the Immigration Reform and Control Act in 1986 making it illegal to hire or recruit illegal immigrants and making employers verify that the person was here legally. Now critics are attacking Trump for saying we need to go beyond that and secure our borders by building a wall. Something, the border patrol agents,

who support Trump, say they need in order to effectively do their job.

> Both Reagan and Trump were passionate about what they believe in.

> Both men are straight-talkers.

> Both were Democrats who became Republicans.

> Both have been TV stars.

> Reagan succeeded Jimmy Carter, a liberal president. Trump hopes to succeed Barack Obama.

> Both desired to 'Make American Great Again.'

> Reagan and Trump both like tax reductions.

> Both are pro-life.

> Both believe in the right of the 2nd amendment.

> Reagan was the first divorced President. Trump has been divorced twice.

Bad company, I think not!

Did you see one of Donald Trump's victory speeches on CNN after a primary win? In his speech, he stated among other things that, "We love the poorly educated." Afterwards, as the political commentators were discussing his speech, and in particular, this comment, you could see them snickering and almost laughing at it. It seemed as if their intent was to mock Trump for saying that. It seemed to me that they were trying, and wanted, to twist his comments into meaning, "Yea right. He loves the poorly educated, because the poor bastards are so stupid, they buy into what he is saying. If they were educated, they would not vote for him. Stupid people." They knew they couldn't come right out and say that, so they just kind of mocked his comments and talked around it, all the while implying it.

Well, I have news for them. The 'poorly educated' people voting for Donald Trump are among the smartest people in the country! They have great instinct and common sense. They are the people who are able to see through the bull, see through the games, and know that they must use their anger to force change upon our country. It is the poorly educated in this country who truly get it. They along with all the other voters, from all demographic groups, are beginning to see what is really at stake here. They just happened to be the group who got it before any of the rest of us. They understand politician 'talk,' and aren't buying it. They understand political commentaries. They understand left wing news and right wing news. They understand the ability for the rich to buy political favors. They understand that everyone comes to the table biased and with an agenda. They understand that what's at stake here is their ability to change, for the better, the course of our nation.

- They are passionate, and they are smart.
- They are committed to change.

- They are committed to a country that works again, for all its citizens.
- They are committed to staying the course, and seeing the change happen.
- They are committed to being proud of America.
- They are committed to seeing an America that works for all.
- And they are committed to seeing our government return to a government for the people, of the people, and by the people. ALL the people.

In the end, the primary thing I have come to realize is – here come the attacks. Attacks, attacks, and more attacks! Donald Trump is being attacked by practically everyone. He is being attacked by President Obama, Hillary Clinton, Bill Clinton, Senator Tim Kaine (Hillary Clinton's VP pick), Anti-Trump Super PACS, Never Trumpers, and the media which give the voice to all his opponents.

The media has become so biased; they have already discarded and convicted him. They are now trying to use the power of the media to convince us to discard and convict him too. We have grown compliant and thought we could trust the media to just report the news. To be unbiased, and fair, to let us ponder and decide who to vote for, but in this election cycle, it is not true. They are using their position to be biased commentators. Watch, listen, and see for yourself. How many say anything about Hillary, except how wonderful, how qualified, etc. she is. Do they talk about all the money she has taken from around the world? How many of them covered the DNC email scandal? How many have honestly covered Bill Clinton and his foundation's ties to the State Department, as recently revealed? Very, very few. The list is long and biased. Just watch the news with eyes wide open.

Donald Trump is also being attacked by some old-guard establishment Republicans. And the list goes on. Doesn't it make you wonder? For me, the more they attack him, the more I'm going to vote for him. Sounds weird, right? The attackers are hoping to convince me through their attacks that he is not the right guy, but the more they attack, the more convinced I become that he is the only person capable of taking their attacks, remain standing firm, and change the broken system. Do we really believe that it was going to be easy to take our country back from the professional governing class?

So much false and misleading information is being put on the airways each day about Donald Trump. I needed a lens to understand it, and a way to understand who was really behind this and why it is happening. Have you noticed, it can even be something as simple as the picture they use? They use one picture that makes Hillary Clinton look all wonderful, and the picture they use for Donald Trump makes him look terrible. They do it on purpose, as a way to influence us, because a picture can be worth a thousand words, as the saying goes.

I would encourage everyone to go online and look up liberal vs. conservative media outlets. The Business Insider has a great article on it dated Oct. 21, 2014, written by Pamela Engel, titled *Here's How Liberal or Conservative Major News Sources Really Are.* It has a graph that labels the news media from 0 neither to -10 liberal or +10 conservative. And a lot of the major news outlets are rated along a continuum in relation to one another. I found it incredibly helpful for giving me a point of reference from which to understand an article I was reading, or a newscast that I was watching, and how potentially bias, one way or the other, the article or show might be.

Mike Huckabee said in a Fox News interview that we are in the middle of a peaceful overthrow of our government and of the Republican Party. The political elite and ultra-rich donors have recognized that the power is being given back to the people through Donald Trump, like it or not. And they don't like it! There has been so much written about how angry Donald Trump voters are and how bigoted they are, but I am not angry or bigoted. However, I do agree that some are. Just **as** some of Hillary Clinton's and Bernie Sander's supporters are **also.**

When Donald Trump came to my town, it was not the Donald Trump supporters who were hitting police, it was people who supported the Democratic Party, who wanted Bernie or Hillary, that were throwing rocks and punching police. One of the people hitting police, was a known gang member. When Bernie Sanders came to town, there were also protests, but they were peaceful protestors. No one hit the police, or beat anyone up as they walked to their car following his rally. So, to blame this all on Donald Trump is reckless and not true. I have a young relative who supported Bernie Sanders, who will not talk to me or go to any family events that I might be at, because I support Donald Trump. I'm actually sad that America has lost its way and is being controlled by a few ultra-wealthy rich people, companies, and their political side-kicks, along with a very biased media.

The goal of this election, in my opinion, is to take back our political process, not to get sidetracked by minor issues. It's like the old saying goes, "When you're up to your neck in alligators, it's hard to remember that the primary objective was to drain the swamp."

Therefore, will I not vote for him because we are being bombarded on the airways with negative ads against him?

With newscasters, political 'experts' and commentaries giving their 'honest' opinion of him? Will I not vote for him because President Obama, said he is "unfit to hold office?" No. I will still vote for him, because I deeply believe it is how God wants me to vote. And once I found peace with my decision; I pretty much now just tune them out. Once I came to realize that it's really about our political process and who currently holds the power, I knew it had to be Donald Trump, the ultimate outsider.

There are no perfect people or candidates in this world. The fundamental question of who runs our country is at stake. The fundamental question of who controls our political process is at stake. The very future of our country, as a democracy, is at stake. The fundamental question of how much power does the ultra-rich have over us, is at stake. The questions of wars, vets, immigration, attacks by jihadist terrorists, our economy, companies leaving the US, the lives of unborn babies, the right to bear arms, and jobs, are at stake. So many more important issues are at stake. It is his ability to speak freely, to talk frankly, to discuss issues openly, that has the ability to once and for all, get all of the elephants out of the room. No one else, can, will, or has the guts to do this.

How We Govern Matters

Matters

Negotiations and
Compromise Are Not Dirty
Words

America is made up of approximately 323 million people. There are only two countries throughout the world, population-wise, that are bigger than the United States. China is home to 1 billion 367 million people (more than four times the size of the U.S.), and India is home to 1 billion 252 million people (almost four times the size of the U.S.).

Of the 323 million people living in the United States, approximately 220 million can vote (per U.S. Census report 2014). However, of those, only 60% of the people who can vote, actually do vote. In recent years due to the gridlock in Washington, the public's dissatisfaction with both parties, voting was and still is at an all-time low. The highest number of voters ever, say they are Independents and refuse to be identified with either party.   Trust in government to be able to solve the country's problems is also at an all-time low, according to a recent Gallup poll.

A country, especially a country that is one of the greatest countries on earth, cannot rule like this. We need an outsider, someone beholden to no one, who will tell it like it is, and who will demand that both sides put down their swords and work together. And if they don't, we need someone who will not be afraid to say, no matter what party it is, who it is that won't come to the table and why. We need someone who knows that America, and Americans, can be excellent. Someone who will turn the playing field on its head, and say we must …. MUST…. do this. We WILL do this. Someone who can excite the electorate, who can give hope again, and who can raise up all people. Someone who has gone around the world, negotiated with some of the best and won. Someone who has actually put thousands of people to work and will do so again. Someone who has identified the problems and is absolutely committed to fixing them. Someone who knows that fighting for what is right and what America needs, won't be easy but can be done. That someone is Donald Trump. However, he needs our help. We must elect people who are willing to go to Washington and find solutions. Who are willing to look at our problems from 360 degrees and find real answers. People who will put aside their party platforms and say, "I am an American first. This is a serious issue, but I know there is a solution, and we can find the answer by working together." Not a solution where only one side wins and the other side lose. Not a solution, where only the ultra-rich win, and the rest of us lose. Not a solution, where one side has to give up all that they believe in and care about. Not a solution where we lock up the majority of black males for drug offenses, and then turn around and continue to allow drugs to pour into our country. We need a solution where both sides win, where both sides keep their core beliefs intact. Impossible, you say? Probably for most, but I believe that Donald Trump and a committed Congress can do this. I believe he is the only one who can force the changes that need to occur. Especially, if we - the people - make it known loud and clear to the Washington politicians that we expect and demand change. That we expect them to quit fooling around with our government and our lives. That we expect them to end the good ole' boys club, to end the rigged professional governing class that has created this quandary and get to work. We pay them to find solutions and work together to implement those solutions, not to throw temper tantrums or shut down our government. And most of all, we expect them to talk about, and find solutions and answers for, THE ELEPHANTS IN THE ROOM, and not quit until they do!

As I mentioned before, when our Constitution was being written, there were huge arguments, vast differences of opinions, fights and bruised egos. The writers of the Constitution knew they could not leave until the job was done. They could not quit, until compromises had been reached, and they found a solution favorable to everyone. This didn't mean that they watered it down, or one side overpowered the other. It meant that they listen to all the views and found common ground. The Bill of Rights, is one such example.   It was not written into the original Constitution, because many felt it wasn't necessary. However, Massachusetts agreed to ratify the Constitution, only if it was agreed that the Constitution, as written, would be amended with a Bill of Rights. New Hampshire, Virginia, New York also ratified it with similar language. They could have said no, held a filibuster, and refused to sign it. They could have stood up and read bedtime stories to their children. I ask you, where would we be, as a nation today, if they had? What if they had walked away, and just let each state be its own country? We would not be who we are or what we have become. Fortunately for us, they found a compromise, a way to make it work for all involved, and we became a country.

A Gallup Poll Survey, taken between Feb. 3-7, showed over 30% of voting Americans considered themselves Republicans; another 30% considered themselves Democrats. The largest group, 37%, are so fed up with both parties, that they have become Independents. In today's world, a person who wants to be a strict Republican or a strict Democrat cannot win the Presidential election. We need someone who can reach across the aisle and engaged people from both parties, and bring the Independents, and the rest of us, back into the process of governing our country.

Jobs, Our Economy, Taxes, and National Debt Matters

I believe we need a President who believes in us, who believes in our country, who believes in our ability to be a great nation here at home. A nation that is great not based on the number of handouts it gives here at home or around the world. But instead is great because we offer the people who live here a chance at a better life. A chance at fulfilling whatever goals they set for themselves. A chance that comes through a fair tax system for all, rich and poor. Not a system that takes from the rich to give to the poor, but a system where the rich also feel that they were treated fairly, and not unduly burdened for the hard work, diligence, dedication, and successes in their lives.

It's so easy for a nation to play Robin Hood. It's so easy to target all the rich as the trouble with America. However, we must remember that not every rich person living in America today, is behind the autocracy/plutocracy/oligarchy form of government that has created the bogged down political politics of today. And many of them are just as much a victim of the politics as the rest of us. Many of them are small and medium business owners who are trying to create jobs, trying to create a livelihood, and are running up against a huge bureaucracy that makes it hard to be in business.

I also think we have to be careful when we say that the top 1% have 99% of the wealth in this country, because when we look at it, it may be true, but what we are not seeing is that their wealth is concentrated into the owning of companies worth billions of dollars. Bill Gates is the wealthiest individual in America. He earned his money by building a company and an industry that never existed before – Microsoft. He got this wealth by being the initial owner of one of the most successful companies in history and taking that company public. He didn't get his wealth by taking it from anyone. Microsoft in 2015 employed 118,000 people. So when we say that it is unfair that so few people, own such much of the wealth, we have to realize how a lot of them got that wealth by creating companies and products of value, not by taking it away from the rest of us. They didn't steal our wealth; they created new wealth for themselves. We need to realize that it's not just sitting there in cash, but is often owned as stock in companies that employ hundreds of thousands of people throughout the world. Or how about Mark Zuckerberg, founder of Facebook? He created something new and took it public. His wealth is tied up in the business he helped create. Facebook in 2015 employed 12,691 people. These two examples, represent two highly successful self-made people. Their wealth came about because of creating a successful product and taking their respective companies public by selling stock to investors. They did not take from the American people to generate their wealth. We absolutely want everyone paying their fair share, but when I saw a Bernie supporter state in an interview on TV that a 90% tax rate for the wealthy was fine with her, so that she could have a free public college education, I was blown away. A 90% tax rate would destroy this country. We really think that people are going to want to stay here and work and create businesses and be productive if we only leave them with 10% of what they earn? This is assuming they are even successful year in and year out. Starting a business is not a guaranteed road to riches. In fact, half of all new businesses fail within their first five years, and only 1/3 are still around 10 years after start-up, per the U.S. Bureau of Labor Statistics. According to a study prepared by the Tax Foundation, the top 1% already pays 34% of all federal taxes. Middle America only pays 20% of all federal taxes. And low income Americans basically pay zero and actually get money paid to them, from the taxes paid by everyone else, in the form of wealth redistribution (earned income tax credits.)

I believe that we should let France be a warning, and an example, for us. France, under their Socialist President Francois Hollande, passed a 75% super tax on the rich in 2012 for a two-year period. It did help fire up left-wing voters, which resulted in ousting his conservative rival, Nicolas Sarkozy. Nevertheless, it failed to deliver the desired results. Even though it raised $420 million euros, it did little or nothing to reduce their $84.7-billion-euro deficit. Some of the wealthy left the country, other just found other ways around the tax. And overall, instead of lowering France's unemployment rate, it increased it. Unfortunately, now outside companies and executives see France as anti-business and are choosing to stay away. In the end, it was deemed by many within the French economy as more harmful to the country's financial well-being, than helpful. It did not result in the end goal of reducing their country's national debt. They have decided not to renew it.

I definitely feel that we should hold everyone responsible for their fair share of taxes, but we should not overtax one group vs. another or make one group responsible for the majority of the costs of our government. That just decreases incentives to work hard and create jobs.

I also believe that we need to stop the back-scratching favoritism that exists among some of the political establishment today, that creates wealth and opportunity for them at the taxpayers' expense. Such as the Clinton's 'Pay to Play' mentality. I believe that if Hillary Clinton is elected President, together she and Bill, will pimp the White House for their own monetary ambitions, just like they did when she was Secretary of State.

One of the best ways to increase tax revenue is through the creation of high-paying jobs. The more people we have employed, the higher the revenue will be from taxes. It is exactly because of Donald Trump's great faith in America, and his experience with creating jobs, his ability to listen to a wide variety of people, that I believe he will be able to help turn this country around and create jobs for all Americans. He understands business. He understands the dilemma and counter-incentives, currently facing a lot of businesses. They would rather keep their money in off-shore accounts than bring it back to the United States to invest because they don't want to lose it to taxes. Apple, CEO Tim Cook, recently stated that Apple would not bring back into the U.S. monies it earned in overseas operations, until our tax rate for corporations are more competitive with other countries. Currently, Apple keeps this money in Ireland which has only a 15% corporate tax rate, vs. the U.S., which is 35%. Trump gets this, and understands what incentives makes businesses tick, what works and what doesn't. That is why his tax proposal included reducing our corporate tax to 15%.

Trump also understands failure. He understands the heartache of having a wonderful idea, of trying to create something from nothing but an idea, and of having it not work out. He also understands that it takes dogged determination and fortitude to get back up and keep on going. He knows that as a country, we need to be competitive with other countries on taxes, regulations, etc. if we want to keep companies that were founded in the U.S. staying here. He has also indicated that in some instances, perhaps instituting a tariff on incoming goods from companies that choose to leave, might be a strong incentive for them to stay.

Carrier Corp, the HVAC manufacturing company, recently stated that they are moving to Mexico because they can no longer manufacture their air conditioners efficiently in the U.S. They stated they were doing so because their suppliers and competitors are moving to Mexico; and that new regulatory requirements are raising their costs and driving up their prices to where they can no longer be competitive. They feel that moving to Mexico will help them operate more cost effectively. However, when U.S. Senator Joe Donnelly asked Carrier Chief, Chris Nelson, exactly which regulatory issues had caused the move, he was unable to cite any! Donnelly stated that the only discrepancy he could see was the differences in pay scale. And I bet you this, that once they move to Mexico, and even with their new lower wages, they will not sell their units for less, they will keep the profits and raise the value of their stock prices. Which will then, I bet, give Chris Nelson a huge salary increase or bonus.

It was widely reported that Carrier received $5.1 million in clean energy tax credits in December 2013. It was also reported; they received $520,815 in incentives from the state of Indiana. And now they are leaving. If Donald Trump was President, and they did receive $5.1 million of taxpayer money, he would call them on the carpet for doing so, and for having the gall to then leave. He'd probably tell them they have to pay it back! There is also, something that all of us can do individually, we should no longer buy Carrier HVAC. It is estimated that 60% of their revenue is generated within the U.S. The consumer can have a great voice, perhaps it's time to voice it.

Donald Trump knows that jobs are important for a country and for its citizens. You will often hear politicians say that a strong military is important for a strong country. In addition to a strong military, Donald Trump understands that a strong economy, with a booming job market, is important for our country. People want to work. They want to have jobs that allow them to care for their families and provide a future for them. When the economy falters, people falter, when families can't care for themselves, when college graduates can't find sustainable jobs, when the only jobs generated are low-paying, part-time jobs, that do not allow people to create a future, they lose hope. When we take a large portion of one race, as we have done with the black population, and put them in jail in large numbers, we just devalue an entire race. By and large, when a person gets out of prison, they are unemployable for life. What do we, as a society expect them to do? We chose jail over drug rehabilitation. We have not invested in any exit programs that could help them find work. We just put people who have been in jail for months or years, back out on the streets, and say, "Have a go at it." What? Yea, like that is really going to work. Donald Trump gets this. That's why he wants to stop illegal drugs from entering at our border, and invest in drug rehabilitation programs.

Sweden is currently dealing with many of the same issues we are regarding illegal immigration, except their problems are due to the refugees coming from Syria. They have a process where they decide if a person seeking entrance from Syria can be allowed to stay or not stay. If they decide the person cannot stay, the person is supposed to leave their country. Instead, the person doesn't leave, and they just go into hiding. Sometimes, they are taken in by churches, sometimes by relatives, or other times by people sympathetic to their plight. The problem for Sweden is this, the illegal immigrants, who Sweden said could not stay and must leave, are not leaving, and they are competing for jobs with the citizens of Sweden. Now, the citizens of Sweden are being pushed out of jobs, because the illegal immigrants are willing to work for less, for no benefits, etc. and a large underground economy is starting to flourish in Sweden.

If you wonder what is wrong with underground economies look at it this way: roads, schools, police, fire, parks, national defense (military), and all other governmental entities, all need to still be paid for and maintained, yet now only the people in the legal economy are paying income taxes. As the underground workers take more jobs, there will be less and less legal workers available to pay for maintaining these areas of societies that make us, Sweden, and countries around the world, modern societies. The more people we have working for cash, and not paying income taxes to support our governmental budgets, the higher our national debt goes or the higher our taxes go, to offset programs deemed essential to the running of America.

Donald Trump also knows that we must create jobs, and we must create good-paying jobs for all people living in the United States legally. To do so, he has stated that we need to lower the income tax on business, and he has stated he would like to see all taxes lowered. There are people out there stating that he wants to raise taxes, this is not true.

If we want companies to stay here and bring back the $2.1 trillion dollars, they are holding off-shore, we have to make it attractive to them to do so. If we want them to pay a living wage to their employees, we have to make it attractive for them to do so. Otherwise, as Carrier and others have shown, they will just pick up and move to a cheaper, more business-friendly, country.

ISIS, Jihadist Extremists, War and Peace Matters

The real threat to countries around the globe from ISIS, al-Qaeda and other radical jihadist terrorist organizations, has grown out of control. Since June 2014, ISIS has superseded in both size and power, other terrorist organizations like al-Qaeda. The main reasons given for this are two-fold, they have access to more money than any other terror organization in history, and they use social media and the Internet to their advantage. Donald Trump is the only candidate who has stated over and over that you have to knock out their income sources - all of their income sources. You have to take away the money they are getting from oil. You have to bomb their stores of cash. You have to go after their money anywhere and everywhere, that you find it, as discussed in the *Why We Need Trump* chapter. He is the only candidate to acknowledge that ISIS is using the banks to their advantage and that this needs to be stopped. Since he has made that statement, a report in *The Telegraph*, by Colin Freeman, entitled 'Islamic State earning millions by playing the stock market' has acknowledged that ISIL is making millions of dollars by playing the foreign-currency markets. Millions of dollars that they use to fund their terrorist activities. Donald Trump has stated that by knocking out their funding sources, and going after their banks, they will subsequently be easy to find and defeat. This makes a lot of sense to me. They currently have money to buy weapons, pay soldiers, take over towns, etc. If you take away their money and their ability to pay for the things they need, you will begin the process of rendering them ineffective. However, as long as we let them have money to carry out their horrible acts, they will continue, and their power will grow.

Donald Trump has mentioned that he will bring back waterboarding, and a lot worse, to use against terrorists - if it is deemed necessary by the military - if it becomes legal to do so once again. To these comments, a lot of people have been horrified. How can we, a civilized nation, do such things? To which Donald Trump replied that ISIS and ISIL are doing things not seen in centuries. They are chopping off the heads of Christians. They are kidnapping and raping women. They are selling kidnapped women for sex slaves. They allow their soldiers to go into towns they have just won and rape women. In addition, in every town they conquer, they proceed to implement their strict view of Islamic law – Sharia. They kill whoever opposes them. They are a serious threat to America and the rest of the world. We are their number-one enemy.

When the revolutionary war was first beginning, it is said that the British soldiers went out to fight in long lines, as was the proper method at the time. The American soldiers, on the other hand, did no such thing. They fought from behind trees, under bushes, in gullies, etc. The American soldiers won the battle that day. What if they had fought the conventional way and had lost? The thing to remember is, ISIS and radical jihadist extremists do not care about rules of engagement, or the proper way to interrogate or not. They do not care about anything, except instilling fear in the world, and being as brutal as needed in order to accomplish their goals. Remember, in the end, they are hoping to convert everyone to their version of Islam, and will kill those who don't. This is not just Christians, but Jews, and people of all religions and faiths, including non-believers, and other Muslim's who do not believe in their strict version of Islamic faith. In addition, they are hoping to speed up the apocalypse, by bringing about the total destruction of the earth. So whatever in their minds, they have to do in order to bring about *'the day of reckoning'*, they will do.

Another interesting point Donald Trump has brought up is this, should the United States of America, a country who is $19 trillion dollars in debt and growing by the second, be the great defender of the world – without any reimbursement from any of the countries that we defend? I think not. If you want to look at the countries that are doing really well economically they do not have large military expenditures. Donald Trump, recognizes that we need a strong military. We just can't suddenly step back from that role, but he also recognizes that the countries we protect have the financial means to help us support our military expenses, and we should ask them for help. I agree. If we implode from our national debt, we won't be able to protect anyone. At the current time, with $19 trillion in debt, it works out to almost $60,000 for every man, women and child living in the U.S., just to retire the debt. That doesn't even include this year's budget deficit. The budget deficit for this year alone is $447,942,612,126 dollars, or about $1,400 for every man, women and child. And remember, it increases by the second. It's amazing to think that our annual deficit and national debt are both so high.

During the primary debates, a question was asked what could be done, if anything, to stop North Korea because they had been launching missiles, as part of a military exercise. Donald Trump was the only candidate who suggested that we needed to ask China to step up and solve the threat. He indicated that China owed us, because we buy most of their products, etc. At the next debate, most of the candidates, when asked this question again, said China can and should help us stop North Korea. They all seemed to forget that Donald Trump was the first one to mention that during an earlier debate.

The main question here is, who is strong enough, forceful enough, determined enough, and stubborn enough, to make the decisions necessary to take on ISIS and radical jihadist extremists and win? To set the policy in place to win? To me only one person, Donald Trump, can do this because God made him exactly that way. Throughout this vicious election process, he has shown over and over again, that he is a fighter. That he will not quit. He is determined and forceful to keep fighting for the causing he believes in.

Great Deals and Tackling Fraud Matter

A country is a business. The business is the governance of the people who live there. How well or poorly that government does, affects everything. If the people who are in charge of the government do a poor job of stewardship with the funds they are given, the people of that country suffer. If the people in charge of the government forget who they work for, the people suffer. If elected officials go into government service with the desire to serve the people, and then get greedy, and go for the money instead, the people suffer.

That is why the backroom deals that a country makes, has ramifications way beyond the corridors of the room in which the deal was made. The citizens of a country, support their government with the taxes they pay. Without taxes, the government could not exist. As our forefathers found out when they first adopted the Articles of Confederation. It gave all the powers to the States, and none to the Federal Government, including the power to tax the people. Without income, the Federal Government could not operate.

How a nation decides to spend its tax dollars, and the deals that nation makes with other countries, its own citizens, and companies around the world, matters. This is why Donald Trump knows that in order for our country to succeed and thrive, we must as a nation negotiate deals that our favorable to us. If, in our desperation to break through to another country's economic base, like China, for example, we agree to stipulations that are not favorable to us as a nation, even if they are favorable to large corporations and the politically connected, we end up economically hurting ourselves and our country. We have done this many times over the years. Our politicians seem to think that America has a bottomless pit of money from which to draw, and they offer everything to other countries. We hand out money like there is no tomorrow. But, the point is, there is a tomorrow. It is our children's and grandchildren's tomorrow. And it's the livelihood of our citizens today, who cannot find a job. And right now, both are at risk of disappearing. We need a leader who will be acutely aware of this with every deal we make. We need Donald Trump, because God designed him to be tough as nail and to stand up for America. God put a desire in his heart, mind, and soul to help America get back to its roots. There are very few people, if any, who could take on the entrenched politics of today and still be standing. Every word he says is twisted and distorted. He is attacked by those who don't want their way of doing business to change. The only way he will win is if we recognize what is happening and stand firm with Donald Trump.

In addition to making sure our interests are protected based upon the deals that we make; we also need to protect our government, our taxes, our agencies, and the people who live here from fraud. To date, Donald Trump is the only candidate to talk about fraud within our government and the need to combat it and reduce it. He has talked about the fraud within the Department of Veterans Affairs and how the abuse and stealing of monies; was preventing our vets from getting the care they needed, and that it must be addressed and stop.

This is a good start, but there is massive fraud on every level throughout every agency in our government. People file false tax returns; individuals abuse their department's purchase order processes; and people take kick-backs for illegally granting contracts to companies. The list and ways people steal from our government goes on and on. In addition, we have crooks in other countries and throughout the world, along with those within our own country, sitting behind computers, stealing peoples' identify, credit card information and bank account funds. These same hackers are stealing this information and selling it to organized crime and other criminal organizations. Fraud is a huge problem and one that must be addressed, and yet only Donald Trump has brought it up. This amazes me.

Per a report compiled by the Heritage Foundation, improper or fraudulent Medicare billings amounted to $47 billion in fraudulent payments. 12.4% of their budget. We need to put our brains and our energies and our talent into stopping fraud, embezzlement, and governmental waste, wherever we find it.   The monies saved could help drastically reduce our national debt. If the average person paid a federal tax rate of 20%, it would take earnings of

$235 billion dollars to just replace the $47 billion that was lost in Medicare fraud in one year! Do you realize how many jobs $235 billion could create?

Secure Borders Matters

Two things Every American Needs to Know about Immigration

Legal Immigration = Good

Illegal Immigration = Slavery, Worker Abuse and Exploitation, and Lower Wages for All

Donald Trump was attacked for his comments about illegal immigrants coming to the United States. He stated that illegal immigrants from Mexico are "bringing drugs, they're bringing crime." He added, "They're rapists and some; I assume, are good people." This was seen by many as an absolutely horrible thing to say. What Donald Trump did, and what he continues to do, is talk about the ELEPHANTS IN THE ROOM. We all know that every day we have people from other countries coming through Mexico to enter our country illegally. California, Texas, Florida, New York, New Jersey, and Illinois have the highest percentages of illegal immigrants in America. Together 60% of all illegal immigrants live in those six states. Unfortunately, people have learned that they can't talk about the issue of illegal immigration without being labeled a racist. What Donald Trump has done for this issue, and so many other issues, is make it okay to talk about them. He made it ok, for American citizens to say, "I have a problem with this." Remember this, Donald Trump is **not against legal immigration**. He is against a border that cannot be contained, because we have absolutely no idea who is in our country. We don't know the intention of the people coming in, as admirable or not, as it may be.

We don't know who they are, if they are coming with drugs, guns, bombs, or black market goods. We don't know if they are being forced to come by drug lords (yes it has happened) who have kidnapped their family or are threatening them and blackmailing them. And, most importantly of all, we cannot protect them, or their children, once they are here. We don't even know where they go, or what they do, once they enter the United States.

Donald Trump's remarks painted people from Mexico with a broad brush, and people were horrified. He did this for hyper-bolt, but the truth is, he didn't just make up the fact that a large number of our drug dealers, gang members, and pimps who are pushing prostitution and slavery are from Mexico and other Central American countries. It has been well documented, but just never talked about. Again, this is not to say that **all** illegal immigrants are bad, the majority **are not**, but our current system is allowing the bad ones to take advantage of our fluid borders and flourish.

As a nation, we cannot ignore the challenges and issues brought on by people entering our country illegally. According to the website, freetheslaves.net, migration from poor countries to richer countries, is one of the main ways that people get forced into slavery today. Traffickers trick vulnerable people by a number of ways, often by posing as legitimate labor recruiters. However, instead of finding them legitimate jobs, they force them into slavery. As stated, 'Migrants are especially vulnerable—they are often very far from home, don't speak the local language, have no funds to return home, and have no friends or family to rely on.'

For the illegal immigrants, not forced into slavery, to find work, they must either work for cash under the table, or they must purchase a stolen Social Security number and fake green card, thereby committing identify theft. This is done, by many companies who are in the illegal business of stealing social security numbers and selling them. For a rather large fee they will "assign" them a social security number and make up false documents, such as a green card, to go with it, allowing them to show that they can 'legally' work in the United States. However, the Social Security number they are "assigned," are actually ones stolen from someone else, typically a child. This act of stealing someone else's identity and using their social security number has huge implications for the child involved and our country as a whole. As reported by The New York Times in the article *Immigrants stealing U.S. Social Security numbers for jobs, not profit* by John Leland dated Sept. 4, 2006, an illegal immigrant used a three years-old social security number to obtain two credit cards and two auto loans with an outstanding credit balance of $25,000. It took her parents over five months to clear the three-year-old's name and her credit history. This is not an isolated case. Every illegal immigrant who wants to work in the United States needs a social security number and a green card, unless they are going to work strictly for cash. There are numerous illegal outfits out there willing to sell them a stolen social security number, and a counterfeit green card. Sometimes, illegal immigrants have had to file for bankruptcy using the stolen social security number. This can ruin a child's credit history before they are even old enough to get a job. In addition to children, there are social security numbers stolen from the elderly, and other venerable people in our society. The article talks about a 78-year-old whose legal records showed she had defaulted on three houses that she never owned.

According to the Pew Hispanic Center, illegal immigrants make up one in every 20 workers in the U.S., and most of them have illegal or fraudulent social security numbers. The rest, work for cash. Each year eight to nine millions earning reports received by the Social Security Administration are filed under names which do not match the name of the person assigned to that number. The majority of which are from people using fraudulent social security numbers. That means that to date, eight to nine million people, including the elderly and children, have had their identity stolen, and someone is illegally using their social security number to work here. Unfortunately, current laws in the United States prevent the Social Security Administration from giving this information to law enforcement, immigration officials, or even the very person who the number legally belongs to! So here we are, spending billions upon billions to "enforce" our borders, yet our own government agencies are not allowed to share useful and helpful information about people who are fraudulently using another person's social security information. This makes no sense to me. It is a felony to falsely use someone else's social security number. Yet, the

Social Security Administration is prevented by law from sharing this information, even though that person is committing identity theft which is a felony, and potentially destroying someone's credit.   This needs to change.

A report found that unauthorized or illegal immigrants from Mexico are more likely, than unauthorized or illegal immigrants overall, to work in the construction industry and less likely to work in services. Construction jobs use to be one of the highly paid blue-collar jobs for American workers. An American worker could earn a living working in the construction trade. Unauthorized/illegal immigrants from Mexico make up at least 75% of the total unauthorized/illegal immigrant population in 10 states: New Mexico, Arizona, Idaho, Wyoming, Colorado, Oklahoma, Wisconsin, Kansas, Oregon, and Texas. California has more unauthorized or illegal immigrants than any other state: 1.6 million people. It is estimated that there were 11.3 million unauthorized immigrants in the U.S. in 2014. Today the number often thrown around is 13 million. It is estimated that they make up 5.1% of the U.S. labor force. In Mexico, the average wage per hour is $4.15. Those who work in agriculture make even less. By coming here, they can almost double their pay. However, while it may be good for them, as compared to their home country, it is very harmful for U.S. citizens and legal immigrants who can no longer find work in construction and other industries because the owners doing the hiring have an easy access to people who will work for less.

So who do you think gets to keep the extra money made on backs of hard-working illegal immigrants? For starters, the owners make a greater percentage of profit, and for two, these same owners can underbid every company that has legally hired U.S. workers and union workers. I have a relative in the construction industry, and he and other companies, who hire union workers, often lose bid after bid, and job after job, because they cannot compete with companies who hire illegal immigrants for low wages, because they have higher labor costs. It hurts them, and it hurts every U.S. employee trying to earn a living; all while the owners of the companies hiring illegal immigrants rake in the money for themselves.

Illegal immigrants will often pay a carrier or "coyote" to transport them across the business. During this process they are often taken advantage of and ripped-off. Once they get here, they have two primary goals: find work so they can send money home and get their family members here, a never-ending cycle of illegal immigration.

The Center for Immigration Studies (CIS) reported in Aug 2015 that illegal immigration had continued to explode. As the present time, per their report, a large percentage of illegal immigrants are now coming from Latin America. Some people try to say that people are coming into the country illegally because it is too hard to get here legally, and we need to make it easier. However, the countries where the greatest number of illegal immigrants are coming from, are also the countries were the most people legally entering our country are coming from. Many people feel that the people who come here illegally are choosing not to wait for their turn, because it is just easier to cross the border and enter our country illegally.

Of those here illegally, roughly 360,000 are known criminals. If we tried to keep them all in jail, it would take 90 prisons, holding 4,000 prisoners each! It would cost billions upon billions upon billions just to house them and hire personnel to supervise them. If instead we send them back to their home countries, and had a secure wall to prevent them from returning to the U.S., the money we would save on prison cost alone would more than pay for the cost of the wall.

Unfortunately, with unsecured borders, "coyotes," drug dealers, carriers, pushers, criminals, and undocumented workers, are able to easily cross the borders into our country. Vulnerable children, without their parents, are also brought into the U.S. by 'coyotes' for a fee, in the hopes of being reunited with family. Instead, they are often taken advantage of once they are here. Along with those who come in only to find work, or to join their families, also comes some really bad, greedy and simply horrible human beings. Human beings that take advantage of children, and force them into child labor, prostitution, slave labor, etc.   It is a sad fact, that anyone who comes here illegally, and is an undocumented or unauthorized worker can, more often than not, be taken advantage of. How can we, a country that stands up and fights for the rights of people around the world, just look the other way on this important issue? Not, closing our border and coming up with a method to document those who are here, and give rights to all workers we allow into this country, results in innocent men, women, and children being exploited and taken advantage of. It needs to stop.

As mentioned, it has been shown, repeatedly, that illegal immigrants, because they are here illegally and without documentation, will work for less than their American counterpart. This brings down wages and jobs for Americans. This is a fact. It's not biased. It's not racists. It is based upon reality. Businesses, at their core, basically want the cheapest of everything, so they will hire the cheapest labor they can find. They will take advantage of people to do that, and, unfortunately, they have the perfect source in illegal immigrants. It seems to me that when we allow people to enter our country illegally, and when we don't really address the issue of illegal immigration, but just look the other way for years and years, we are supporting the exploitation of the undocumented workers. It's like on one hand, we want to say, terrible, terrible, and on the other hand, we secretly wave them in.

The Federation for American Immigration Reform (FAIR) in their study, *Human Trafficking – Exploitation of Illegal Aliens,* found that between 14,500 - 17,500 human beings are being deceived and exploited by fraud and other means into illegally entering the United States **each year**. It is estimated that there are approximately, 60,000 people held in captivity as **slaves** in the U.S. today. Read that again, 60,000 people being held in captivity as slaves in the U.S. today! That is terrible. Have we forgotten the Civil War? Once here, they are forced to work under brutal and inhumane conditions. Women and children are forced into commercial sex operations, prostitution, stripping, pornography, and live-sex shows. Others are forced into domestic servitude, sweatshops factories, and agricultural work. Add it up, year after year, and we have a huge problem.   For more about this issue go to http://www.fairus.org/issue/human-trafficking-exploitation-of-illegal-aliens.

Instead of actively doing something about it, we want to argue about the inhumanness of building a wall, while supporting a 'fence.' How is knowingly letting criminals take advantage of innocent people and force them into a life of slavery, humane? That's why I like Donald Trump, and I believe God wants me to vote for him. He is a doer, a person who tackles issues head on. He will keep at it until he finds a solution for this problem.

There was also an article in The Guardian, dated March 28, 2013, written by Paul Harris, located at (https://www.theguardian.com/world/2013/mar/28/undocumented-migrants-worker-abuse-deportation),   which found that another way illegal immigrants who work here are often taken advantage of is through the refusal of companies to pay them for work performed. The article tells the true story of how a group of construction workers, who were in the country illegally, had performed work for which they had not been paid. They complained to their boss about not being paid, but instead of paying them, their boss called the police and officers from Immigration and Customs Enforcement, and they were all arrested, they never did receive the wages they were owed or promised. Some Americans, will say, "Ha, that will teach them to come here illegally." But what does that say about us as a country? As a nation, we are willing to send our young men and women off to wars in other countries to fight against the exploitation of people, while we willingly sit by and allow people, in our own country, to be abused and exploited.

Unfortunately, there are employers out there who willingly and purposely hired illegal workers with the set purpose and intention of never paying them their full wage and threatening them with deportation if they complain. This also is a form of slavery and exploitation. They are either not paid for work done, or not paid in full. Sometimes they are paid just enough, to keep them coming back and working until the job is done, with the promise of fully paying them in the end. Which then doesn't happen. They are also forced to work for long hours, in inhumane working conditions. They cannot complain because they do not have the proper documentation to work in the country legally, and their bosses know that more than likely they are working using a stolen social security number and a fake green card. Companies take advantage of them for their own greedy financial gain. Worse of all, is that our elected officials have known about this for years. Yet, they refused to solve the problem. That is why, I believe that God wants me to vote for Donald Trump. He knows that the problem must be solved, and it must be seriously tackled starting with the wall.

When it comes to the deportation of millions of illegal immigrants, I haven't formed an opinion on that yet. I know that there will be a back and forth between the President and Congress on this. I know that Donald Trump is going to start from a position of 'deport them all!' knowing that in the end, in order to get a compromise that works, there will be give and take. But like Marco Rubio stated during his campaign, we can't even have the discussion, until we have the wall, and our borders are secure. I anticipate that while the wall is being built, people who are here illegally may decide on their own to quietly leave with their families, before the border is closed off. It has been found that when President Obama spoke favorably about amnesty and a pathway for citizenship for illegal immigrants more illegal immigrants came into the country. Whenever the talk shifts to not forming a pathway to citizenship, less entered our country illegally. After the amnesty programs of 1986, put in place by Reagan and

Bush, illegal immigration increased as more people were hoping we would do it again.

Rep. Duncan Hunter, a California Republican, appropriately assessed the situation and said, "The greatest existential threat to this nation right now is this administration's open-border policy. This is no longer about immigration; it's about the President and DHS keeping open the corridors on the southern border that are accessible to anyone in the world. We can defend our country against another country's navy, a missile threat and even repel a conventional military invasion. But the President's policy of allowing anyone into the nation as students or refugees presents a serious threat." People from Pakistan, Syria and other countries, where known jihadist extremists are known to originate, have been found coming into our country illegally, through our southern border.

Do you want to know what $45,000 will get you? A 2017 Audi Q7, a Jaguar F-Pace, or if you're an ISIS jihadist *entrance* into the U.S. through Mexico. Yep, it really is that easy. Once you're here, you don't have to worry about finding a job, the ISIS organization has already given you money for a place to live, a car, etc. You just have to blend quietly in and wait for orders. It is estimated that ISIS brings in between $1 - $2 million *a day* from oil sales alone, that would be enough to send an estimated 10-20 jihadist extremists into the U.S. each day. They, of course, have other things they use that money for, but they also have multiple sources of money. According to a 2014 New York Times investigation, since 2008 al-Qaeda and its affiliates brought in $125 million from ransoms alone. In 2013, they earned $66 million from kidnapping people and threatening to kill them, unless their families or governments paid up. They then used this source of money to fund their criminal activities and capture more people. With an estimated 7.125 billion people in the world, there is an endless supply of people to capture and ransom money to be paid. This is an issue that has not really been talked about by politicians, and has not made it into the news very often, making it seem like it is not true. Nevertheless, it is very, very true.

Heck, the $400 million President Obama secretly gave to Iran in cash for, uh, crumbling infrastructure, like roads, bridges, buildings, could have funded the entrance of almost 8,900 jihadists. Calm down, media, I'm not saying it did, I'm saying that potentially that cash could have been used for this, or guns, or ammo, or bombs, or… because see that's the funny thing about cash, you can never really tell where it went. But as we've been told by White House spokesman, Josh Earnest, it went to improve crumbling infrastructure, and maybe some of it went to "nefarious activities." Crumbling infrastructure, and other types of things, that countries everywhere, pay for with cash. Here let's see; I owe you $100 million for this road, hold on a minute while I get my forklift over here with the cash on it.

Now, let's count it out. I don't know, but somehow this scenario, just isn't working for me.

What if I told you about a country that allowed drug dealers, and convicted felons, to enter multiple times with impunity? A country that allowed thousands of tons of illegal drugs to enter without stopping it, even though that country had spent millions, if not billions of dollars, for 45 years on a "war" against drugs. A country that has put millions of its own citizens in jail (mostly blacks) for using drugs during that time period. A country that has never come up with a way to help its addicted citizens get un-addicted. A country that ABSOLUTELY can stop a large part of the illegal drugs coming into this country by building a secure wall, along the main border, where the drugs enter from, but will not. Well look at the following facts because this country is us.

During a July 21 Judiciary Committee hearing on crimes by illegal immigrants, it was noted that in 2014:

✓ 193 illegal immigrants committed homicides.
✓ 426 committed sexual assaults.
✓ 16,000 had drunk-driving convictions.
✓ 87,381 committed other crimes while in America.
✓ That makes a grand total of 104,000 illegal immigrants who were allowed to remain in the U.S.,

even though the law states they should have been deported.

✓ Currently, the Director of ICE said they have a backlog of **500,000 cases of people who should have been deported for criminal activity**, and not allowed to return, but are still here!

In 2011, the Government Accountability Office reported that we had:

> ❯ 25,000 undocumented immigrants serving sentences for homicide.
> ❯ 42,000 serving time for robberies.
> ❯ 70,000 serving time for sex crimes.
> ❯ 81,000 serving time for auto thefts.
> ❯ 95,000 serving time for weapon's offenses.
> ❯ 213,000 serving time for assaults.
> ❯ Children of immigrants have been found to commit crimes at rates substantially higher than their parents. (This is a statistical report – not racism.)
> ❯ Illegal immigrants, while being approximately only 3.5% of the populations, were 20% of the kidnapping/hostage taking sentences in 2014.
> ❯ Illegal immigrants were ¾ of the federal drug possession sentences in 2014.
> ❯ Tijuana is one of the most dangerous cities in Mexico due to drug trade and human trafficking.
> ❯ Corruption is growing and running rampant on **both sides** due to the amount of money involved.

Hillary Clinton and company, say Donald Trump is a racist because he talks about illegal immigration. She claims that when he talks about illegal immigration, he is attacking everyone who has ever immigrated to the United States. That whenever a person talks about illegal immigration, they are slamming all immigrants. In my opinion, this is so far from true. As a nation, we should be able to talk about the issue, about people, wherever they come from, who enter the country **illegally**. We should not be labeled racist, because we want to find solutions for this issue. We should not be labeled racist because we believe that a wall will be more secure, than the fence that Hillary Clinton voted for.

It seems to me, it's so convenient and self-serving for Hillary Clinton, the Democrat Party, and the media to leave out the part that he is only attacking the ***illegal*** way people from Mexico and other countries have entered our country. He is not attacking legal immigrants, and he is not against immigration. We are all well aware that everyone migrated or immigrated to the United States, even the Native American Indians who got here first, migrated to this country. However, he is taking issue with the fact that for years people from Mexico, and other countries, have been circumventing our legal immigration process and entering the US by crossing our southern border through Mexico illegally. He is also attacking the fact that we have proven and reliable intelligence telling us that radical Islamic terrorists have infiltrated refugee camps, with the explicit purpose of coming here to carry out terrorist attacks. Just as they already have in other countries around the world.

It's true that Donald Trump does speak out against those people **who illegally** enter our country with drugs and with the purpose of committing crime. However, anyone who has followed Donald Trump, also knows that he is not against all people from Mexico or all people of Hispanic heritage. Nor is he against all Muslims. The people who support him and follow him know that he made his statements as a hyper-bolt for effect. Why? Because he wanted to get America's attention. He has gone on the record many times stating that he understands why people from Mexico and elsewhere wants to come to America. However, he wants them to come here **legally**. Yes, he wants to build a wall, but he wants to also have a mechanism in place for allowing people to legally enter into the United States. Is that racist? I don't think so.

I believe when you actually listen to the words Donald Trump speaks, and not to the analysts or oppositions' interpretation of what Donald Trump said, or the hand-picked 20 second sound bite that fills the airways, or the many terrible names he is being called by Hillary and company, you will find that he is not a racist. HE is NOT against immigration. He is NOT against people from Mexico; he is NOT against Muslims. He **IS AGAINST** illegal immigration, crooks, criminals, drug pushers, drug dealers, rapist, murders, thieves, pimps, jihadist extremists, and slave owners, who can come in freely through our unprotected borders and harm our citizens, our country, and harm the illegal immigrants that came looking for work through exploitation and slavery.

I really can't emphasize this enough, talking about illegal immigration is not racist, and it doesn't mean that everyone who ever came to the country illegally is a terrible, rotten, no-good human being. Donald Trump knows this. If fact, in his book, *Crippled America*, he acknowledges that most of them are great people, who are trying to make a living for themselves and their families. Illegal immigration, is one of our elephants, that must be talked about and dealt with.

Why Hillary Can't Do What Trump Can

There are a few really strong reasons why I will not vote for Hillary Clinton, and why I believe she cannot do what Donald Trump can. I have listed them below.

✓ Number 1. She is the ultimate insider. She and Bill have used their political power to rake in millions and billions of dollars from around the world to benefit themselves, their foundation, and their daughter. Money donated from the ultra-wealthy, in my opinion, does what money has always done, buy access for those who want something.

There is one story in the bible where Jesus got really angry. And it was when he saw the money-changers and animal-sellers in the temple. He drove out all of those who bought and sold inside the temple; he overturned the tables of the money-changers and the seats of those who sold pigeons. He said to them, "It is written, 'My house shall be called a house of prayer' but you make it a den of robbers."

Unfortunately, here in America, our nation's capital has become a place that is bought and sold, and political favors doled out. Mutual back-scratching occurs, and inside deals are made. It is no longer a place that represents the people. It has become a place filled with lobbyist of the wealthy and well-connected. Run by plutocrats, and the professional governing class, for the benefit of the few. That is why for people who don't really get it, what Donald Trump did by not taking donations during the primary race, was his attempt to give us back our country. This is huge.

✓ Number 2. Under a Hillary Clinton presidency, there will be no real change in America. She has already said this during her campaign. She wants to continue on with the way things are. The rich, the wealthy, and the well-connected will continue to control our political system. There have been real issues raised about the money given to the Clintons and their foundation. And serious questions raised about fundraising campaign issues and not abiding by the spirit of the law for her *Hillary for America* campaign.

✓ Number 3. I think this bears repeating, there will be NO real change in America. Our **illegal** immigration issues will not be solved. Our national debt will not be reduced, and instead it will be increased due to the additional new give-away programs. Sustainable living wage jobs will not be created. Compromise with members of Congress will not be reached. Thoughtful considerate legislation, with input from both sides, will not occur. The potential for terrorist jihadist attacks, here at home, will become worse as we allow refugees to enter knowing that we have a limited ability to properly vet and screen them due to the war in Syria. Corruption and fraud in government will increase.

✓ Number 4. I believe, the Clintons feel that they are smarter than the rest of us. Example number 2 above, when they created a mechanism to circumvent the true intention of campaign finance laws. And remember when Bill Clinton said, "I did not have sexual relations with that girl." And said he answered the question honestly, because it depended upon one's definition of the word: "is." Please....

✓ Number 5. Remember, Hillary Clinton's biggest backers are the ultra-elite, ultra-rich, and Wall-Street hedge-fund/political power brokers that have rigged the system against average Americans already. Why would we want to give them four more years of power?

✓ Number 6. I believe that she truly does not want to unite the country. She is using words to divide the people and the parties. When she, and her backers, use these totally false and unsubstantiated words to describe Donald Trump – demagogue, fantasist, misogynist, racist, narcissist, fascist, isolationist, bully, and liar, and then says she above name-calling, she is trying to divide the country with fear and hatred. She continually demonizes Republicans and their beliefs. This is not uniting the country.

✓ Number 7. It has been well documented that her husband, unfortunately, cheats; which isn't her fault at all, and breaks my heart for her. However, there are a number of claims by some of the women involved that she tried to bully them into silence. She and Bill deny this, duh. Just look at what happened to Monica Lewinsky. Why was she the guilty party and Bill innocent? Why did she have to leave the country in shame? She was a young, impressible girl, who the

President of the United States made a pass at. Why did they put all the blame on her? Nevertheless, it doesn't stop with Monica; several other women have come forward. Their story is often the same. One of the people even wrote a book about it, Dolly Kyle Brown, an attorney, wrote about her long 20+ year affair with Bill Clinton in her book, *Hillary the Other Women: A Political Memoir*. One of the attorneys, that was the chief investigative counsel for Clinton's impeachment, wrote the forward for the book and vouched for Dolly Kyle Brown's character. He stated that had the impeachment gone forward she was one of the key witnesses who would have been called upon. He wrote his own book titled *Sellout: The Inside Story About Clinton's Impeachment*.

✓ Number 8. Is Hillary Clinton really a champion for women and the LGBT community? If you listen to the stories of the women that her husband had sexual relationships with, you have to at the very least question this. And if you read about the story of how she defended a rapist against a young innocent 12-year-old girl early in her career, you must question this. If you look at the hiring practices of *The Bill, Hillary, and Chelsea Clinton Foundation*, you must question this. If you look into the hiring practices of her own campaign for President, you must question this. If you look at some of the countries where she, Bill, and their foundation have taken money from and how those countries treat women and LGTB members, you must question this. Remember, actions speak louder than words.

✓ Number 9. We are a nation in debt, and instead of decreasing our debt, she has proposed program after program that will increase it, in an attempt to appease voters and win votes. She preaches about a give-away economy, (primarily as a vote getter, I believe) not a strong, individual life aspiring, fulfill your true potential economy.

✓ Number 10. America needs a change. We need to get back to the country, that President Kennedy talked about when he said, "Ask not what your country can do for you, but rather what you can do for your country.' Under the current democratic leadership and agenda, we are anything but this. We have gone into debt trying to be all and do all to everyone around the world.   We have let political cronyism, and inside favoritism decide many of our economic decisions. This is not sustainable.

✓ Number 11. Hillary Clinton supports a world economy, instead of a strong American economy. This is why she has supported, and will continue to support, trade agreements that favor other countries more than our own. Her view of America is more in line, with a one world view, without borders, and large corporation rule. Donald Trump's view is of a strong, healthy, working, productive America.

✓ Number 12. She works the system for her own financial gain and benefit. As mentioned, while

Secretary of State, she traveled around the world; while Bill Clinton, and their family's foundation raked in millions upon millions upon billions of dollars from among others, oppressive regimes that degraded women, children, Christians, and its own citizens.

✓ Number 13. The DNC was hacked, by whom no one knows for sure. In some of the released DNC emails, it was shown that the DNC purposely did a number of things to sabotage Bernie Sanders primary campaign. The DNC purposely and willingly subjugated the will of the people, to get Hillary Clinton the nomination. No wonder that even though Bernie Sanders was filling arena and stadiums, and Hillary Clinton was not, Hillary Clinton magically won.

✓ Number 14. Hillary Clinton, came out and blamed the DNC hack on Donald Trump and the Russians. Stating that they were trying to back Donald Trump and influence this election. Hold the phone! For one thing, the assertion is absurd. For another thing, the Russians didn't invent the emails. The content of the emails stands on their own merit. Hillary and the DNC are trying to deflect the content of the emails and what they did by saying those darn Russians, they caught us red-handed. Let's blame Trump! Let's not address the issue of us sabotaging the election from Bernie Sanders, and let's put it all on Trump and the Russians. That is so wrong on so many levels.

✓ Number 15. I believe, that for Hillary and Bill Clinton, the end justifies the means. They will do whatever, say whatever, to get the end results that they want. In my opinion, they think that they are above the law, and above the will of the people.

    ✓ Number 16. In the end for me, it came down to an issue of faith – my faith. I believe that God wants me to vote for Donald Trump. Yes, he can be very outspoken and yes; he can be very politically incorrect, but underneath it all – he is running for the right reasons. I believe that Hillary Clinton is not. She has a record of bending the laws (besides her recent campaign finance laws, other people have written about a long list of instances, going way back to Arkansas), she willingly takes large amounts of money from people around the world, and she basically will say or promise anything that is needed in order to get elected. Donald Trump, on the other hand, stands up for what he believes in. Yes, even to the tune of 3500 lawsuits. He stands and fights for what he believes in, not because he is trying to rip people off, but because he believes strongly enough to hire lawyers and take it before a court. Do you really think a person, who is trying to rip people off would go to court?

Unfortunately, Bernie Sanders has chosen to ignore all the serious, character-flawed reasons he gave during the primaries as to why he was against Hillary Clinton. He is now supporting her, even though it has come out that the DNC purposely and willingly sabotaged his campaign. And even though it was shown that Hillary Clinton sabotaged and purposely circumvented campaign finance laws to fund her *Hillary for America* campaign to the tune of $264,374,319! At the opening of the DNC Convention, Rev. Leah Daughtry stated in her remarks, the DNC was a party of "We the people." How can she honestly say that, knowing that her party, the Democratic party, purposefully and willingly sabotaged the campaign election of Bernie Sanders? And knowing that it was the Democratic Party, and President Bill Clinton, that pass the *Violent Crime Control and Law Enforcement Act of 1994*, resulting in millions of black men being jailed for drug addiction, rather than receiving the help, they needed to overcome it? Once jailed, at a rate three times that of white Americans, they were basically unemployable for life. Is it any wonder that black Americans have not made progress? This does not sound like a party for the people. How can the Democrats, be the party of 'we the people,' when for years they have supported and encouraged single black women to get an abortion, instead of seeking alternative care for the mother during her pregnancy, with adoption of her child, once born? Between prisons and abortions, the Democratic Party has decimated the black community. Report after report shows that the black community has not made progress in years. I can only hope, that the people listening, will judge for themselves the validity of these arguments, and look at them with fresh eyes.

In addition to my reasons, here are the reasons Bernie Sanders gave during his campaign as to why Hillary Clinton was not the person to become our next President.

    ✓ Taking hundreds of thousands of dollars from Goldman Sachs as payment for private speeches – up to $225,000 per speech.

    ✓ Representing the top 1% through donations to her Super PACS. And through raising $25 million from special interests, including $15 million from Wall Street.

    ✓ The use of Super Delegates to tie up the lead in the primaries before the elections even took place.

    ✓ The EXPLOITATION of campaign finance law to use money raised for her *Hillary for America* presidential campaign. The fact that she skated campaign finance laws and raked in millions, which was supposed to be given to states, but was spent on her campaign instead. Per Jeff Weaver, Bernie Sanders campaign manager, these actions allowed people like Alice Walton of Wal-Mart fame, George Clooney (I know...bummer...he's so darn handsome...) and other super-wealthy backers to skirt the legal limits of campaign contributions.

    ✓ Her judgements – during the primaries Bernie Sanders, frequently questioned the Secretary of State's judgement.

    ✓ Her foundation – taking money from foreign governments and companies in Russia, many of which are dictatorships while she was Secretary of State.

✓ Bernie Sanders stated that Hillary Clinton, in his opinion, was not qualified to be President, because "she through her Super-PACS was taking tens of millions of dollars in special-interest funds."

✓ He continued that she was not qualified because she "supported the Panama Free Trade Agreement...which has allowed wealthy people all over the world to avoid paying their taxes to their countries."

I would ask every person who is going to vote in the 2016 election, to very carefully look over this list. Donald Trump has not done even **one** of these things. So, I must ask you who among the two candidates running for President of the United States, has the better character and values? Who is the one person, who has not exploited our political system for their own financial gain? Who is the one person, who through their companies, promoted women into leadership positions before it became popular to do so? Who is the one person to actually give equal pay to women? Who is the one person to promote people based on ability not degrees or political connection? Who is the one person who has stated again, and again, and again, that he does not need the job, but is taking it to represent the American people and make sure that our interests are put first?

I doubt that Bernie Sanders' supporters will even see, let alone read this book. But, I hope that they remember and think about the things they heard Bernie Sanders say during the primaries, and decide, was Bernie

Sorry Hillary! God Wants Trump!!

Sanders just blowing hot air when he made those statements or did they mean something? Are they true? Are they valid? Or can they just be washed away for a few items listed on the DNC convention platform?

Why Voting for Trump Matters

Right now, our country is in the middle of an important crossroad. As a nation, we are having some very important and difficult discussions that will affect our future for years and decades to come. We have future Supreme Court nominations and appointments to make and agree upon. We still have drugs pouring into our country from our southern border, as if someone was transporting milk. And as a nation, our response so far to the issue of drugs is to lock up those who get addicted, rather than stop the drugs from entering. We punish users with jail time instead of give treatment to those addicted. Donald Trump would like to see a two-prong approach, stop the drugs and give treatment to those addicted.

Anyone and everyone can get into the United States and bring with them whatever they want. People, drugs, weapons, goods to sell at undercut prices, and so on all pour across our border. Our own citizens (especially children and the elderly) are having their identity and social security numbers stolen so that illegal immigrants can find work. I think that most of the illegal immigrants using stolen social security numbers, probably don't realize the extent and seriousness of their actions. They may not even realize they are stolen numbers, but it still does not make it right. We need and deserve a government willing to address these important and difficult issues.

We have companies that were founded in America leaving and going to Mexico and elsewhere. However, these very same companies still expect us to buy their products, even though they have deserted us. We have companies, founded here in America, that are keeping millions if not billions in cash, in countries like Ireland, due to our repressive 35% corporate tax rate. Donald Trump wants to change this. He wants to make us competitive with the world once again.

We have a very viable and serious threat from al-Qaeda/ISIS/radical jihadist terrorists, as do Muslims, Christians, Jews and people of all religions everywhere. We cannot ignore the fact that al-Qaeda/ISIS/radical jihadist terrorists from around the world have very clearly stated that they want to destroy us and destroy our way of life. Even after 15 years of fighting, we have not been able to defeat them. Al-Qaeda recently wrote an online article urging 'lone wolves' to take up arms and target "areas where the Anglo-Saxon community (in the U.S.) is generally concentrated." There is now an online jihadist network, a virtual group known as al-Fajr Center, that has centralized the online jihadists movement. It takes propaganda from a variety of jihadist groups, including al-Qaeda and ISIS and distributes it out across forums and message boards which it controls. They have tens of thousands of members, which give them a wide reach to targeted radicals, extremists, and jihadists everywhere. They also use the al-Fajr Center as a large online recruiting center, that works 24/7 with hate filled messages to cast all non-Islamic, non-believing nations, as their enemy. They aim their message at the disenfranchised, disillusioned, young men and women around the world. They tell them they will receive the "great reward of martyrdom." According to the religious text of Islam, this would be 72 virgin maidens in paradise for each male martyr, and for females the promise of an eternal spouse. In addition to their online efforts, they send operatives into the United States and other countries, trying to recruit people to their radical beliefs and thoughts. The primary goal of ISIS/al-Qaeda/radical jihadist terrorists is to encourage recruits to take up arms and kill anyone they deem to be an "infantile" their neighbors, co-workers, and innocent citizens, in countries and nations throughout the world.

In the midst of this, one candidate has stood up, and said that this was wrong. He has said that we need a wall so that only legal immigrants can come in. He has stated that we need a wall, secure enough, to keep out the illegal drugs and goods that are destroying our country. He has also said that we need to stop radical Islamist terrorists from entering our country. He has stated that our current vetting process isn't working, and until we can figure out how is it, that ISIS supporters and radical Islamic terrorists, who want to destroy our country, are coming in we may need to **temporarily** ban people coming from terrorist areas. Hillary Clinton has attacked Donald Trump on not knowing about ISIS, yet he made his comments about not being able to properly vet Muslim immigrant's months ago, and it just came out the end of July, by the FBI Director,

James Comey, that this is true. FBI Director Comey stated that we are not able to properly vet the 10,000 Syrian refugees President Obama wants to let into the country. So, if Donald Trump knows nothing, how did he know this, months before James Comey admitted it?

Donald Trump was attacked and questioned during the DNC about his knowledge of the Constitution, and publicly asked if he had ever read it because of his suggestion of a temporary ban on Muslims. Guess what? Per numerous legal scholars, Donald Trump was absolutely correct. He cannot keep out legal U.S. citizens, but he can TEMPORARILY ban others he feels are a risk to America by letting them in.

Under U.S. Code, the president does have the statutory authority to keep anyone out of the country, for any reason he thinks best. Per 8 USC §1182

"Whenever the President finds that the entry of any aliens or of any class of aliens into the United States would be detrimental to the interests of the United States, he may by proclamation, and for such period as he shall deem necessary, suspend the entry of all aliens or any class of aliens as immigrants or nonimmigrants, or impose on the entry of aliens any restrictions he may deem to be appropriate."

For this, he was labeled a racist. He was labeled as being ignorant, and someone who did not know our Constitutional laws. Absolutely, not true. His speech was labeled as hate speech. It's not hate speech. It's the speech of a person who is concerned for the safety of our country. He has stated over and over that he likes Muslims, he just doesn't like terrorists. His point was, as a nation, we have got to figure this out. His statement was meant to be a hyper-bolt moment, to wake the country up. He was willing to talk about a serious problem, another elephant in the room; which is that ISIS had illegally obtained passport printing machines, and now has an entire fake passport unit, that will legally allow them to enter our country, or any country, easily.

Almost every week, there is a new terrorist attack in France, Belgium, Germany, and elsewhere. It has been reported by Europol that has many as 3,000-5,000 trained jihadists, posed as Syrian refugees, and are now dispersed throughout Europe, waiting for the right time to conduct a terrorist operation in the very countries that were willing to take them in. One captured ISIS smuggler revealed that ISIS had already laid-out ambitious plans to use the refugee crises to infiltrate the West. We cannot take this intelligence information lightly. We cannot overlook, or down play it, or assume that we have the capacity, technology, or means to thwart any attack on U.S. soil by trained jihadists before it occurs. It seems to me, that we would be better off to support in-country refugee camps.

Like the ones, Donald Trump talks about, where we give them the supplies, food, housing, etc. that they need, until we can reliably come up with a system to identify who the radical jihadists are hiding in their midst, or until we can end the Syrian war. Once the war has ended, they would have the option to return home to the country they love, and help rebuild it.

In the midst of all of this, we have one candidate, Donald Trump, willing to stand up and talk about the elephants in the room, and because of this, every anti-Trump Super PAC, the Democratic establishment, old-guard Republicans, Never Trumpers, and a large part of the media, along with Hillary Clinton, have thrown label after label against him in an effort to stop the truth from coming out. Every day, as I learned more and more, and as more and more is revealed about Hillary Clinton, it becomes clearer and clearer to me why I heard a nudging from God to do this book and to proclaim that God, wants Trump for President. Donald Trump, even with all his issues, even with his big mouth, his loud voice, his portrayed lack of sensitivity, and his lack of political correctness, has used his campaign to talk about the real issues existing in America today. He has not tried to circumvent our election process, and he has not tried to undermine the will of people to have their say on election day. When we were founded, we were founded on the principles of one nation under God. One nation. The Democrats want you to believe that Donald Trump and Republicans are trying to divide up America. It is not true, when he talks about creating jobs, he talks about jobs for all Americans, when he talks about illegal immigration, he does so because he realizes that pay in America, for jobs for Americans, will not go up, unless cheap labor and slave labor is removed from our country. (Just as Bernie Sanders realized this too.) He realizes that we cannot allow our national debt to skyrocket anymore, to levels so unsustainable that we very soon we will not even be able to pay down the interest on our loans, let alone the debt itself. When he talks about other countries paying for their fair share of NATO, as originally agreed to, it is because he realizes that one of the most important ways to decrease our debt is to reduce our expenses. Why do we, a nation, with the highest rate of debt in the entire world, keep funding other nations? When he talks about redoing or rewriting trade agreements, it is not because he is against one group of people or another. It is because he is for Americans. He is for a strong America, where our citizens – all our citizens – can enjoy the freedoms that our country has to offer and can reach their full potential in life.

I can only ask you to seriously think about what the DNC did to Bernie Sanders campaign, go online here http://www.thegatewaypundit.com/2016/07/detailed-list-findings-wikileaks-dnc-document-dump/ and read their racist, demagogue filled emails, and realize that the same trickery and lies they said about Bernie Sanders, they are doing in a much worse and bigger way against Donald Trump. In my opinion, Hillary Clinton and the Democratic

Party do not deserve to be in the White House. Before the primaries even took place, they decided who their candidate was going to be. Do you realize the implications this has for future elections? Even if you do not like Donald Trump, if even you hate Donald Trump, I hope you realize how important this message is to send to the Democratic Party and all elected parties within our country. At this point, in my opinion, a vote for Hillary Clinton, is a vote for the continued corruption of the American political system. This is not hearsay; this has been proven by their own emails, coming from their own political campaign committee and the people who run it. It has been shown and proven by the words that they themselves wrote. It cannot be denied or blamed on anyone, other than themselves. In my humble opinion, they sold out America, and one of our most sacred rights, to elect our government officials, as representatives of the people, who will be for the people, by the people, and of the people. This is something, that cannot be overlooked or forgiven. If it is, politics in America will never change and each of our votes will be meaningless. The soldiers who died here at home fighting for the formation of a better union, or those who died far away in a foreign country trying to give others the same rights to vote for their representation, have all died for what? Seriously, for what?

As mentioned numerous times, please just remember, as the hate-filled, unfit for office, twisted lies and rhetoric hit the airways in the last few months, that contrary to what the Democrats want you to believe, Donald Trump is for a strong America, a flourishing America, an America where everyone can reach their full potential. He knows that in order for this to happen, we must have strong borders so that we are in control of who comes in, when they come in, how they come in, what they bring in, and how they are treated once they get here. To me, this is not a racist position. This is a protectionist position, from a person who wants to protect America.

We can say all we want about how we are going to fight ISIS and other radical jihadist terrorists. We can say how we are going to protect America; how we are going to fight the 45-year-long war on drugs (that under President Bill Clinton's *Violent Crime Control and Law Enforcement Act of 1994*, has locked up more Black Americans than any other law in history); how we are going to create jobs; and how terrible it is that American companies are leaving America for foreign countries. But until we ACT - that's all it is – just talk. Politicians love to talk, they love to tell us what they are going to do, and how they are going to do it. In the meantime, because the Republicans refuse to play with President Obama, he just says, 'Ok, I'll do it on my own,' very similar to the 'Little Red Hen.' And what we end up with is something very one-sided and to the left. After which, the Republican leadership comes out and says, 'How terrible! President Obama is a dictator!' And yet, because the Democrats on the other side, are also unwilling to bend, the Republicans are left with no choice, but to stand their ground. Neither side, is willing to find common ground. Isn't it amazing, that here we are in America, the 'greatest democracy on the face of the earth,' and our elected officials cannot find common ground with one another? It's time to shake them up by sending an outsider to Washington.

I strongly believe that if Republicans and Democrats *remembered* who the Constitution says they work for, the people who elected them in the first place, if they *stopped* listening to special interests and big money, if they *engaged* in the process for the benefit of the American people – all the American people, they could find some common ground.

How can we even pretend to be peace makers around the world, when we can't even reach a compromise here at home? How can we set an example for other countries on how to govern when we can't set an example for ourselves? How can we proclaim, look at us, a republic with a democracy, where the people have a vote, and a voice is the way to go, when, in reality, what we really have is an oligarchy, run by a lot of unwilling to bend either way politicians – who have an overall approval rating of only 20%? How can we prove to the world, that as a country, we are not corrupt given the DNC email scandal, and all the money raked in by the Clintons?

I strongly believe, and now know, that Donald Trump is the only person who can turn our country around and bring us together. He is the only person running who is not and has never been a politician. It is time to send a message to Washington that we, the citizens of this great country, want our nation back from the oligarchy that has ruled it for too long. We want it back from the ultra-rich, the special-interest-groups, from the far right, from the far left, and the professional governing class, who thinks that America was made for them, and only them, and who in turn use our political process to enrich their own pockets.

Just like in Rome long ago, the professional governing class, the plutocracy/oligarchy that rules today, want to keep on ruling. Do you honestly think that the ruling class of America, is just going to give up the system that has benefited them so well, easily? It has been reported that President Obama wants to go around the world, giving speeches and collecting millions in speaking fees, just like Hillary and Bill. Well, in order to do that he needs Hillary in the White House. After all, what does he have to say worth millions, except his connection to the President of the United States, and his personal insights that this connection provides? No one should use the White House as a means to become ultra-wealthy. Our democracy, our country should not be up for sale to governments and dictators around the world, even if done under the guise of a charitable foundation or speaking fees. No President, other than Bill Clinton, no other high-ranking governmental official, other than Hillary Clinton, has ever done this. When Hillary Clinton became Secretary of State, Bill Clinton doubled his speaking fees from $250,000 to $500,000. What did he have that suddenly doubled in value, other than access to his wife and the State Department. If she becomes President, will his fees double again to $1,000,000? It's unthinkable to 'sell' America to dictators, other countries, and multi-national rich corporations and high-powered executives.

It has been stated that Donald Trump's candidacy has inspired a revolution in America. Where the working class and millions of people actually believe that they can have a voice in America again. Where they believe that the American dream still lives, outside of political office. Meaning that it doesn't just exist for those who want to run for President or political office and become rich. You cannot have a revolution without strong attacks against the person heading the call for change. They will continue to throw everything they can at Donald Trump, and sometimes because he is not part of the professional governing class, or an experienced politician, he will put his foot in his mouth and help the media out. I strongly suspect that between now and the election, we will see very few news reports that are favorable about Donald Trump. The press is too liberal and too much in the back pockets of the ruling class to allow for that.

Look if they sabotaged Bernie Sanders, who they supposedly liked, well come on, they hate Donald Trump. In their minds, Donald Trump is worse than Bernie Sanders. Unfortunately, it is not about democracy, folks. It is about the governing class, the class that knows better than its citizens, how to rule America. The existing plutocracy/autocracy will not go quietly in the night. They have way too much at stake for that. Wall Street, has too much at stake, for that. The professional governing class, who wants us to lean to the left, and become more socialist in nature, has too much at stake for that. The media, which by and large belongs to the Democratic party and leans to the left, wants to keep their party in charge. Only, the voters who are behind Donald Trump and want real change can do anything about this, but only if we vote in such large numbers that a clear mandate is given to Washington.

Let's quickly summarize, why Donald Trump and this movement/revolution are the enemy. For the Democratic Party, it's simple. He is not Hillary Clinton. The one current politician, who has according to report after report, an article after article, used governmental service, along with her husband, more than any other person in the history of our nation, to enrich themselves. Ruling America has been good for the pocket books of the ruling class. For the rest of the elected officials, and ultra-rich plutocracies, they know that Donald Trump is not indebted to them, and will go out and do what is right for the country, whether they like it or not. They know he will stand up to China. He will secure the borders. He will ensure that our military fights, and really fight, ISIS (not a Vietnam War type fight). They know he will encourage companies through a number of measures to return to the U.S. to create, jobs, jobs, and jobs. And they know he will build the wall, thus ending our source of cheap and slave labor, along with illegal drugs. And most of all they hate his supporters, because we have figured it out.

It's true he does not know the game or the language of politicians. He makes bold statements that are politically insensitive in trying to get his ideas across. He does not have years of political experience, during which he has learned to speak like a politician. Which means to talk in circles, offer a spin, and never offend anyone, and pretend you are going to give everyone what they want.

I'm sure that what scares them the most is that he is a doer. He likes to accomplish things. He is willing to compromise. He is willing to think about what is best for America, not the world. He will not favor large world-wide corporations over American business. He will not favor Wall Street and big money in politics over Americans. He will not send our young men and women needlessly into other countries just to destabilize them. He is willing to talk to both sides. He is willing to reach compromises in an attempt to move us forward, in an attempt to get something done for once in Washington. He uses words like compromise, making a deal, working together, **getting**

things done for the American people. He is unequivocally proud of our military and police forces.

I mentioned previously about all the U.S. companies that want into China and elsewhere around the world. They followed the cheapest labor, wherever it led. Just as now, they are leaving China and going to other countries. We also know that in order for technology companies to go into China, they are required to give the Chinese government all their secret source codes, submit to invasive audits, build in back-doors, etc. According to one copyright industry association, the piracy rate in China remains one of the highest in the world (over 90 percent), and U.S. companies lose over one billion dollars in legitimate business each year to piracy. In addition to this, as Donald Trump has tried explaining over and over again, they along with other countries, manipulate their currencies, so they can underbid us. It's kind of like a double whammy. They manipulate their currencies so that U.S. companies cannot compete with them in manufacturing, and then on top of that, Chinese companies counterfeit our products. Doesn't it seem like this should make "Made in the USA" really attractive?

I believe that China and other Asian-pacific countries will continue to do this, until someone is bold enough to say, wait a minute. China is four times the size of the U.S. They have four times the workers. Their wages are significantly lower than ours. They subsidize their companies with all kinds of financial incentives and money. They can, and probably will, end up with the largest army in the world. They already have the world's largest manufacturing economy. It is only a matter of time before they become the number one economic and military force in the world. They are already maneuvering to take over islands and other areas, in that part of the world. And what are we doing? Oh yea, I forgot we are making trade deals in their favor. Man, we are such a nice country!

With this as our backdrop, it has become clear to me that a large number of our elected officials are not looking out for the best interest of the American people. Did you realize that if you want to become rich, run for Congress? If you want to become ultra-rich become President. It's true.

I believe that individuals currently in power, along with their ultra-wealthy backers, know there will never be another Donald Trump. So now they are throwing millions of millions of dollars against him. And calling him every name in the book, in hopes that something will stick. To date, and we have less than three months to go, Hillary Clinton has raised $374,333,383 in her bid to "buy," err win the Presidency. Read that number again, $374,333,383. Wow! For a job that pay $400,000/year. It would take 936 years to earn that much money as President of the United States. Clearly, the rich understand the power and influence that position holds. I believe, their reasoning is this: by defeating Donald Trump, they are also sending a powerful message to any future candidates – "Stay within the lines and play by our rules. The people do not run America. We the ruling-class know what is best for America."

For those in command, it truly is not about:

- ➤ US, the people of the United States.
- ➤ JOBS, at least not our jobs.
- ➤ ISIS, national security, and protecting America from radical Islamic extremists
- ➤ DRUGS, both prescription and illegal. How many millionaires in the U.S. have made their money, one way or another, off of drugs? Think about it. Big Pharma sells their drugs, like OxyContin, to the doctors and hospital as the painkiller of choice. These are highly addictive meds, there is no plan to wean the person off of the drug, they get hooked, when they can't get off, and can't get OxyContin, they turn to heroin.
- ➤ BUILDING WEALTH for middle class and lower class Americans. How many families in America have seen their wealth, and their lives destroyed, by drugs since the War on Drugs began? How many people of color, but predominately the black community, have had their lives destroyed by being sent to jail for drugs? Remember, jails don't have drug rehabilitation programs. And remember the big push to jail drug offenders was started under Bill Clinton's Administration.

➢ UNFAIR TRADE AGREEMENTS that are hurting our country's economy and jobs. They don't care about the average worker in our country – they only care about their company's bottom line, the current value of their stock, their stock options, their offshore accounts, and their ability to increase their own personal wealth.

➢ HEALTH CARE. Does anyone even remember that Donald Trump took on the entire Republican establishment, when he said he wanted health care that would ensure that people who couldn't afford health care, wouldn't die in the streets?

➢ GUNS and the 2nd amendment. If a person wants a gun, they will find a way to get a gun, with or without gun control. Criminals don't follow laws, let alone gun control laws.

➢ INFRASTRUCTURE, they may care a little about this - if they can make lots of money from it. As long as they don't have to pay for it.

➢ TAX CODE, this will be a non-issue with Hillary in the White House. It will continue to be in favor of Wall Street and not main street.

As you think about who to vote for, please remember this: Donald Trump is the only person still standing, who individually stood up and said; we have a corrupt system, and it is working against 99% of all Americans. We need to fix it. Donald Trump ran his primary campaign without Super PACS, and without taking any of their money. He did this so that he was free from obligations and bribery. He was free to get his message out there. He was free from the rich aristocrats on both sides, who have for so long controlled politics in America. This is why, he truly is the only candidate free to work in the best interest of the American people - all the American people.

I know I have said this over and over, but it is so important, so one last time: remember Donald Trump, did not try to subjugate the will of the American people by trying to influence how the Democratic voters feel about Bernie Sanders. He did not try to take away the will of the people to have a fair and open election. The DNC did that. This alone, should be reason enough to vote for Donald Trump. It's time for the citizens of our great country to take our country back and make America Great Again.

The truth has now come down to this: Who is America really for?

✓ It is for the people who run Wall Street and give Hillary Clinton $225,000 for an hour or less speech?
✓ It is for a few families who think it is their divine right to rule America? People who believe that the end, justifies the means, no matter how crooked or dishonest?
✓ It is for the ultra-rich who can donate millions upon millions to Hillary Clinton's campaign and

to pay for negative ads aimed at Donald Trump, because a million to them, is like a dollar to us?

✓ It is for people who want to make their career, retirement, and ultimate road to riches, being an elected professional politician?

✓ It is for those who want to take, but then deny other Americans what they get? Remember, by and large, every elected official who goes in Washington, or works in state, county, and city governments across this country, will end up with a nice big fat retirement, complete with health care.

✓ Make no mistake about it the democratic elite, along with some very, very, wealthy people want to control America. They know a win by Trump will mean the American people will win, and they will be out of controlling the country.

✓ What does this mean if Trump doesn't win? It means same ole same ole. It means that Wall Street still controls the purse strings; government handouts/bailouts will be the order of the day; open borders will rule low wages and stagnant job growth; slavery inside America will continue; interventionist policies around the world will continue to destabilized countries and regions.

✓ In the end, as shown by the emails from the DNC (a supposed non-biased arm of the Democratic Party) this race is a race about democracy. A race about the very values our country was founded on. We cannot let the controlling political parties ruled by the ultra-rich, the power brokers of Washington, and the elite families win. There will never be another Trump. There will never be another person, bold enough, brave enough, stubborn enough, and loud enough to take them on. The time is now. Do not let the negative, untruthful, and biased ads sway you. Do not let the money of others who are trying to buy votes - win. Do not let those who want to control the future of America to benefit themselves - win. Please do not let them make this a race about the shock-affect things Trump says, or the "presidential" vs. "non-presidential" aspects of his race. It is about so much more than that. Yes, I know that sometimes he needs to keep his mouth shut. Yes, I know that sometimes he says what he shouldn't, and yes, I know that he attacks back when attacked. And it seems he has a propensity for answering every question put to him, when sometimes he should take a pass. But, I have come to strongly believe, that a lot of this is just the way God made him. Do you think a reserve, always politically correct person, would have had the guts to stand up against the enormous odds Donald Trump faced, and say what needed to be said? Remember, he went it alone for most of this election. He was at times actually fighting both parties. Why, because no one wants to give up power. The political ruling class like it there, and they like all the perks they get from lobbyists, etc. They don't want us changing up their normal ways of doing, or not doing, business. They know under Donald Trump; change is a-coming.

✓ There has never been a race, and will never be another race, in our lifetime, as important as this one. This race is for the people, by the people, and being driven by one man and the people who believe in him. Bernie Sanders tried and failed. Donald Trump is the only voice left standing for the people.

Please stand up and bring the political process back to everyday Americans. We fought the Revolutionary War for precisely this reason, because we wanted to be a country for the people, by the people, and of the people. We did not want a few ultra-rich people controlling our destiny. Unfortunately, 240 years after our birth, it has happened again, but this time it's not the British ruling class; it's our own political establishment. This isn't the first time, and I'm sure it won't be the last. The question, is what are we going to do about it?

What I have come to realize is that God made Donald Trump, so uniquely that never again will there be a Donald Trump. If Donald Trump loses, no other person will be willing to use their own money to run their campaign in order to not be obligated to anyone, just so they can stand-up for the people – for ALL the people of the United States, for whites, Hispanics, blacks, Christians, Muslims, Asians, American Indians, and on and on. Nothing will change. It doesn't matter if a Republican is in the White House or a

Sorry Hillary! God Wants Trump!!

Democrat. No one can do what Donald Trump can do. No one else can send a loud and clear message to both parties, that the good times of mutual back-scratching is over. Partisan politics are over. That leveraging the future of the United States, for the few, is over. So, I say once again, the most important thing to come out of this election – is the very future of our country. It is time to send a clear and unequivocal message to the leaders of our country, to politicians, Super PACS, political commentators, and the media – that WE AREN'T GOING TO TAKE IT ANYMORE – WE WANT CHANGE!

We are not going to take

their politics,

their favoritism,

their lack of care for veterans,

their willingness to let companies leave the United States,

the complicated, ridiculous tax systems filled with special interest deals and steals,

their method of treating an elected political position as a lifelong job,

their willingness to do the bidding of the rich in exchange for money, gifts, and other perks,

their willingness to let our infrastructures decay
and crumble until people are hurt and die and lawsuits
finally make them fix it,

their willingness to let other countries walk all over
us,

their willingness to not talk about the ELEPHANTS
in the room because it awkward and not politically correct,

their willingness to let criminals just walk right in to
this country with their drugs, their guns, and their desire
to destroy us,

their willingness to think they, along with the
special interest, the powerful elite, and ultra-rich, are the
only ones smart enough to rule America and to decide its
fate – WITHOUT input from the American people,

their willingness to not protect our right to bear
arms,

their willingness to mess with the economy, as if it
was their boy toy,

their willingness within the Democratic Party's own
political machine, to not honor their commitment to stay
impartial until the peoples' voices are heard and the
primary election is over,

Sorry Hillary! God Wants Trump!!

their willingness in the media to let their own personal biases and views, taint, twist and spin everything they report

their willingness to send millions upon millions upon millions of dollars to a country known for supporting and growing terrorism, known for wanting a nuclear weapon, known for its leader stating that he will wipe Israel off of the face of the earth. And while we are doing all of this, our elected officials are fine with sending our sons and daughters off to fight the war on terror. How does this work exactly? If you are funding the enemy, that supports those you are fighting?

For these reasons and many, many, more

the time to stop this is NOW!

The way to stop it is by voting for the one candidate with the guts and fortitude to stop it.

DONALD J. TRUMP.

As a footnote: I recently watched some of the Democratic National Convention. I watched Bill Clinton talk about Hillary. And I actually feel some sadness that I am not voting for her, but I know from all that I have learned that I cannot. It seems to me that somewhere along the way Bill and Hillary Clinton, have lost their way. It seems to me that politics for them has become more about the money they can earn, than the people they serve. I realize that more than making history with the first women President; we must take this, once in a lifetime opportunity, to get our country back to its roots. It is just as important, at this critical moment, as it was when our country was first formed, the very essence of what it means to be the United States of America is at stake. Please don't get conned by the targeted 'promises' that aim to 'buy' your vote. Stand up for the 99% not the 1%.

Please join me in voting for

Donald J. Trump

for President

on November 8, 2016.

Together we can take back our country.

Thank you!

www.ingramcontent.com/pod-product-compliance
Lightning Source LLC
Chambersburg PA
CBHW060334290526
45793CB00003B/616